Olga Goloveshkina
COLORING BOOK

Magic horses

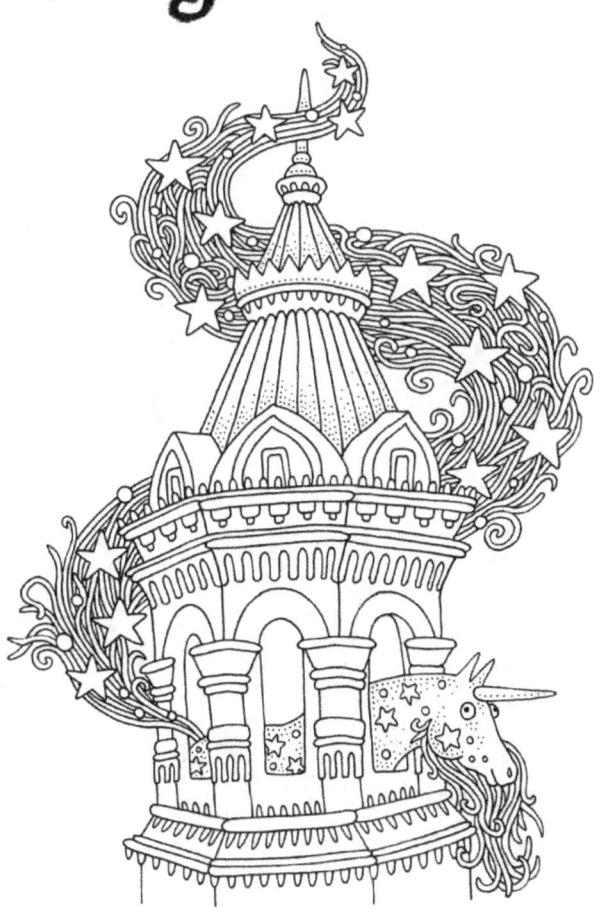

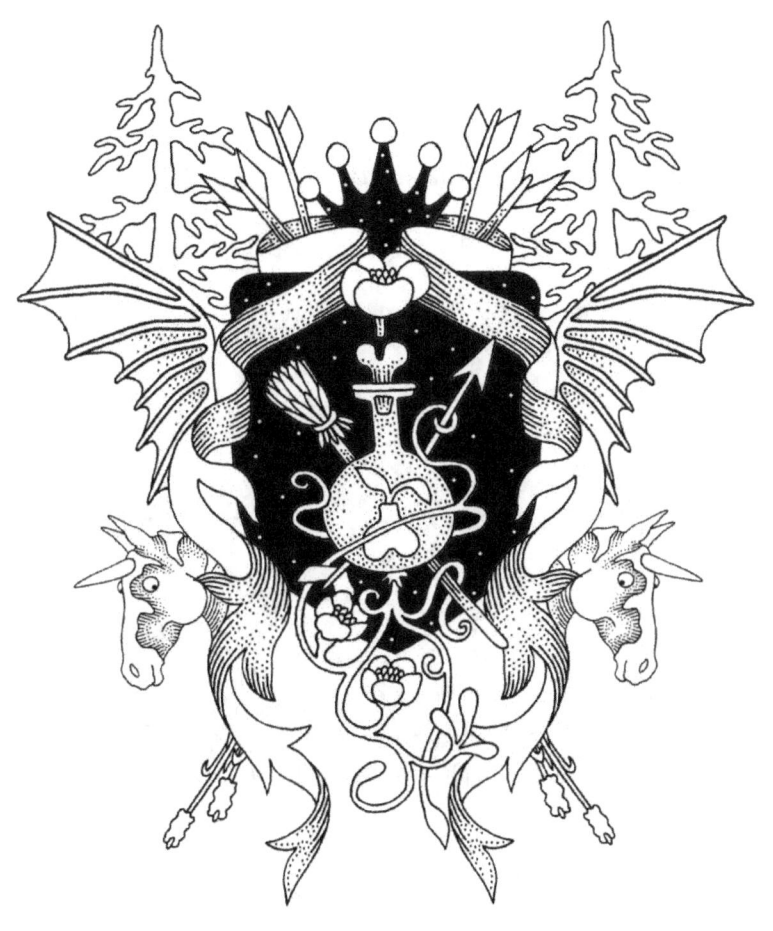

This book belongs to

Thank you very much for choosing this book.

I sincerely hope you enjoy it.

I tried very hard drawing her.

Your feedback is very important to me.

Reviews of my books on Amazon
with your pictures help me a lot.

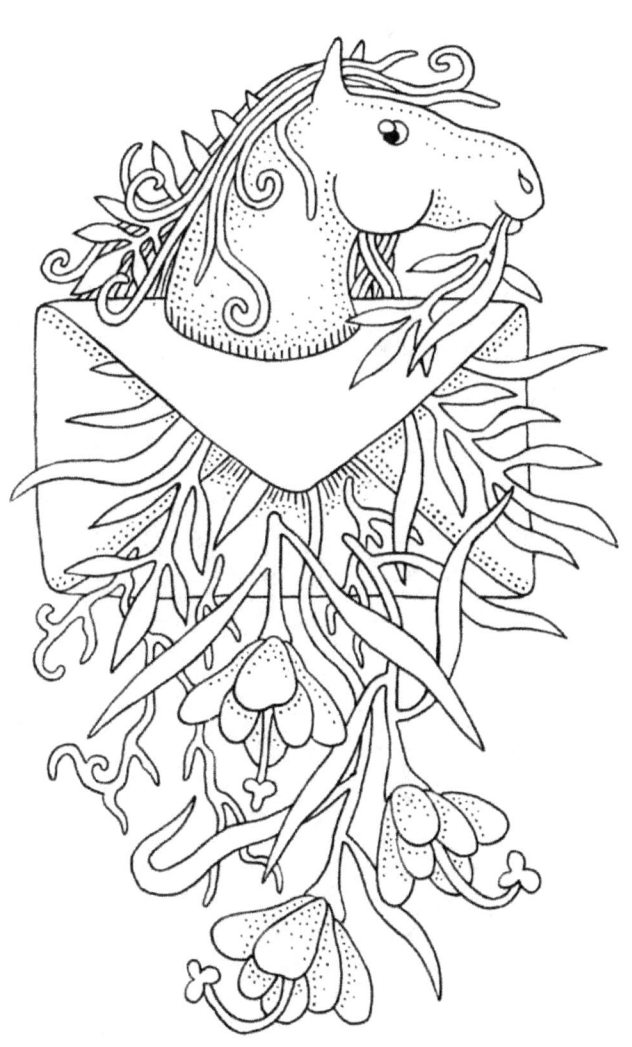

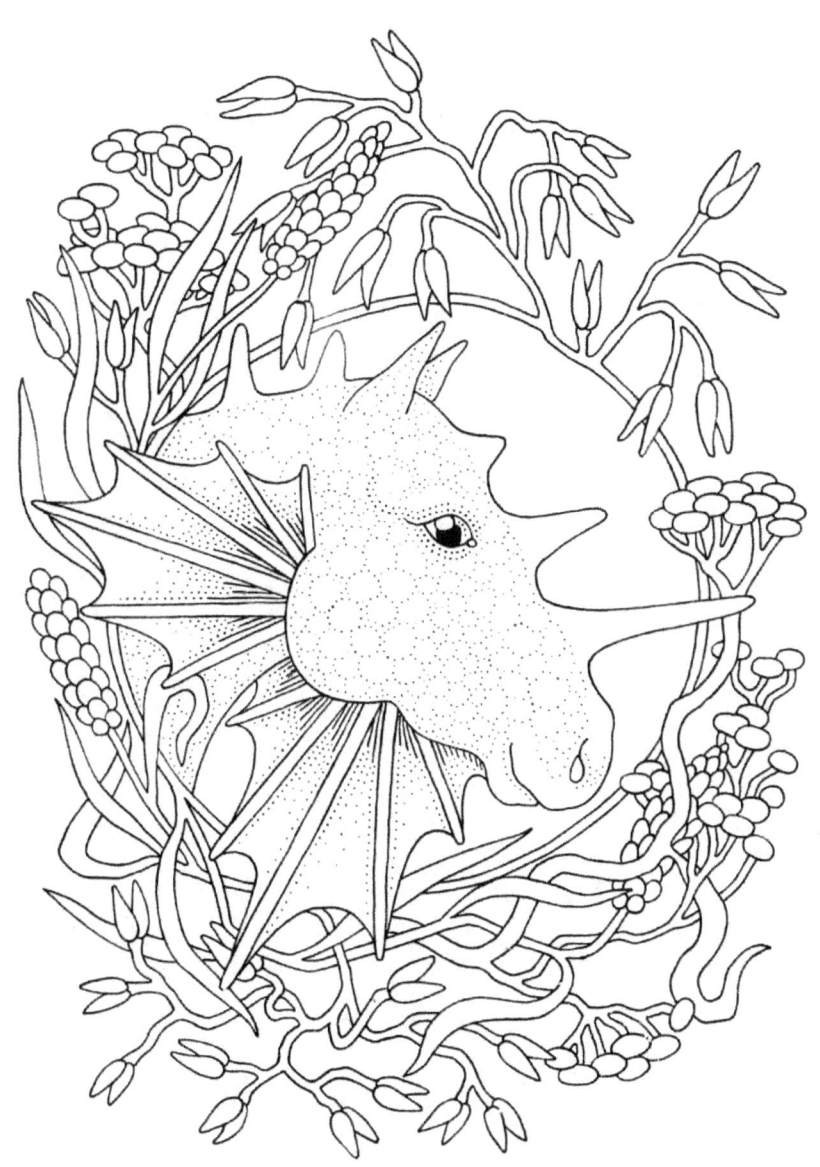

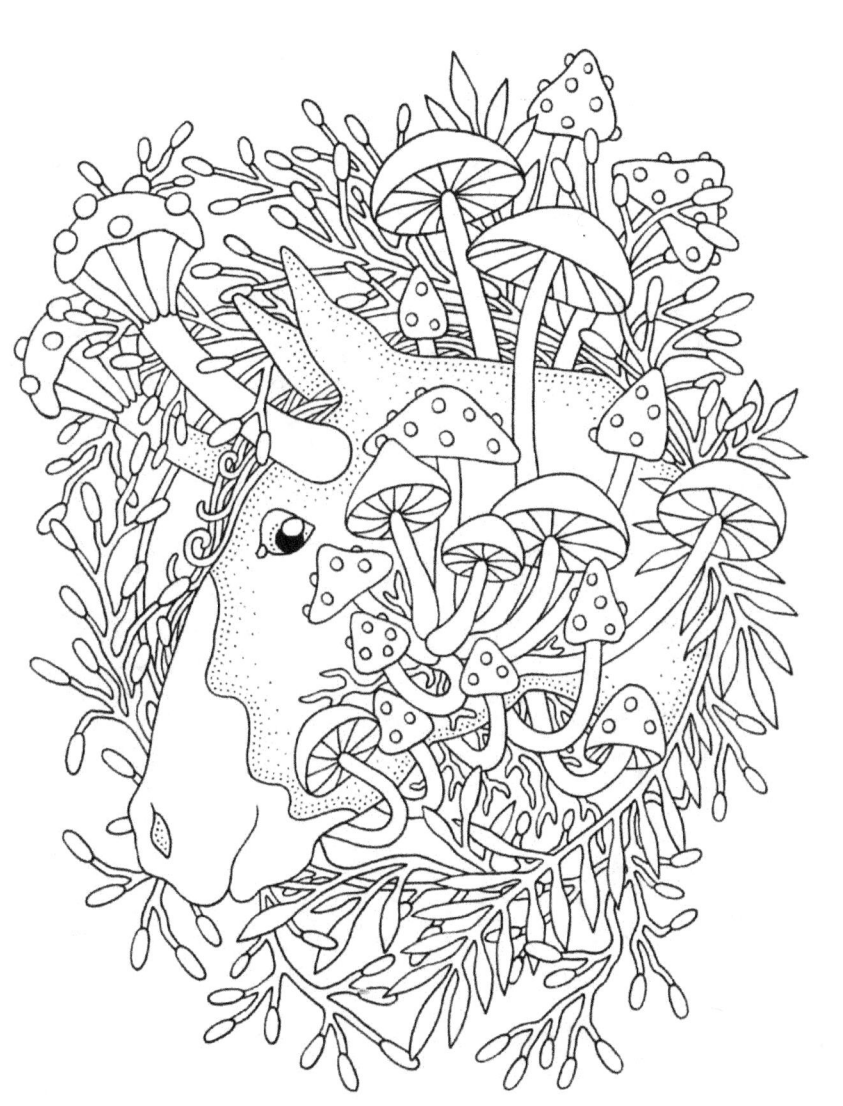

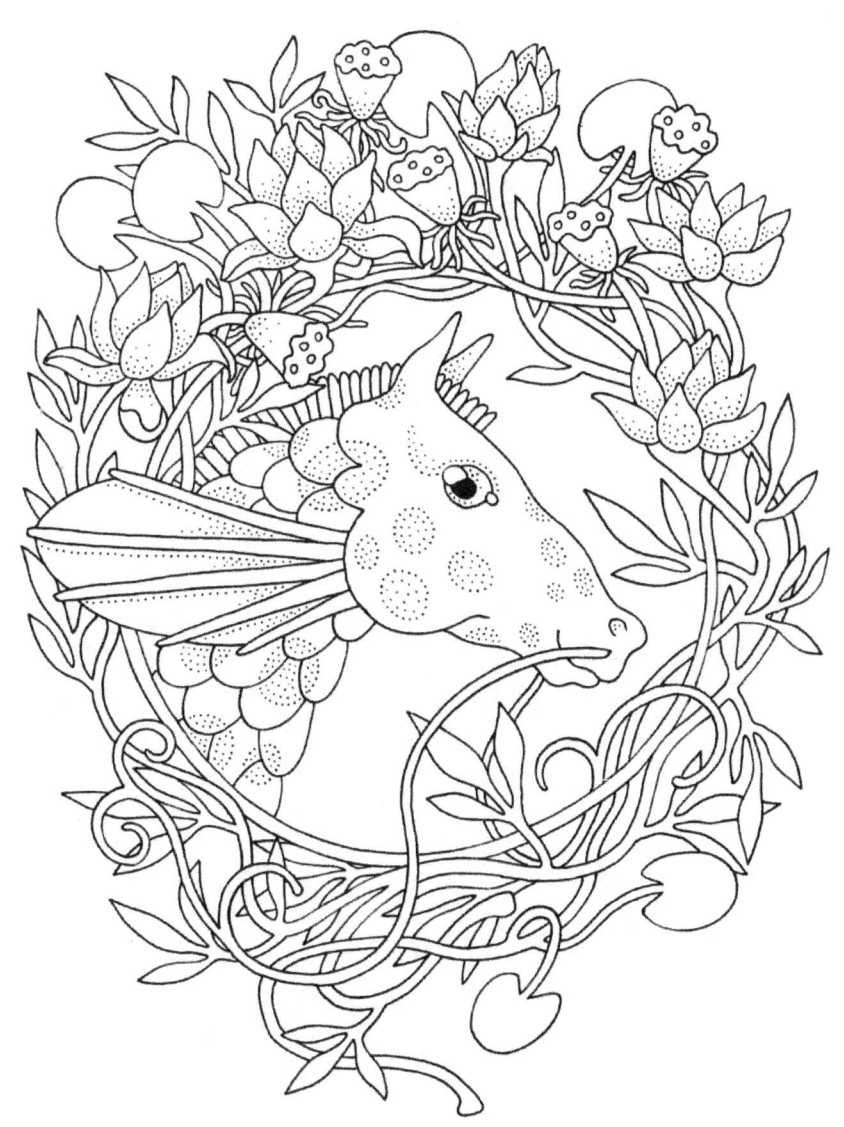

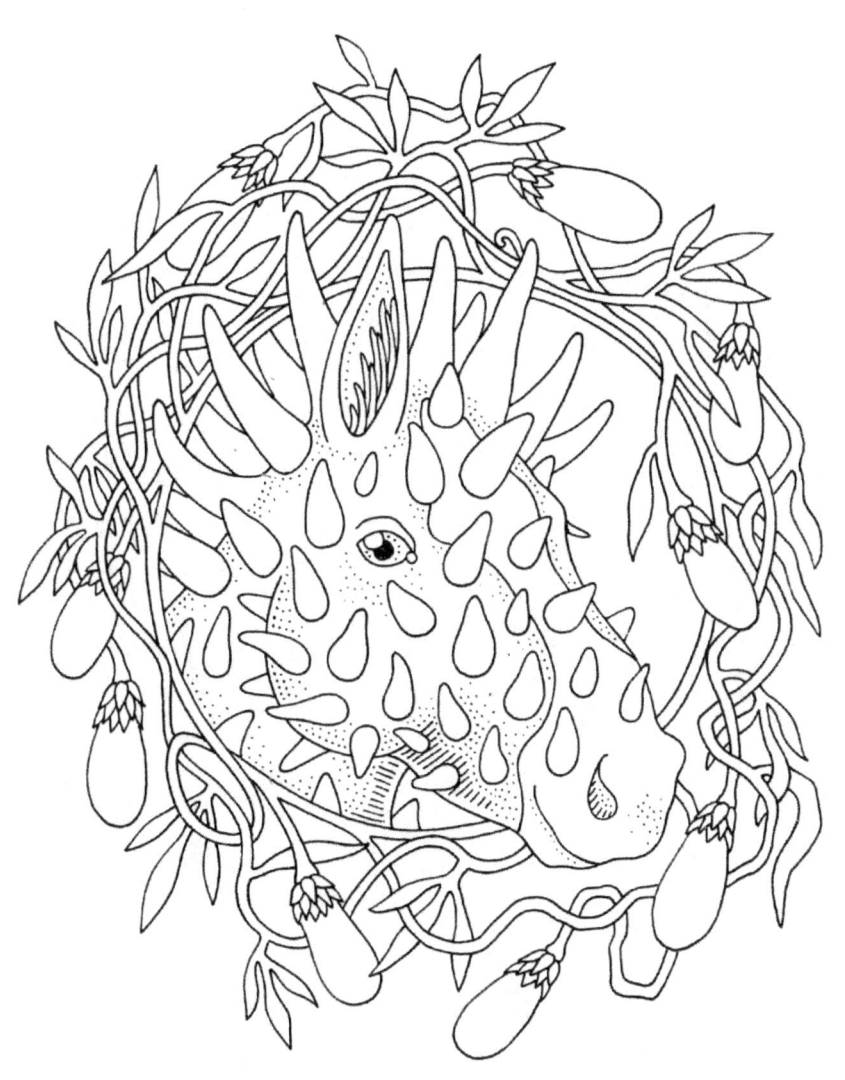

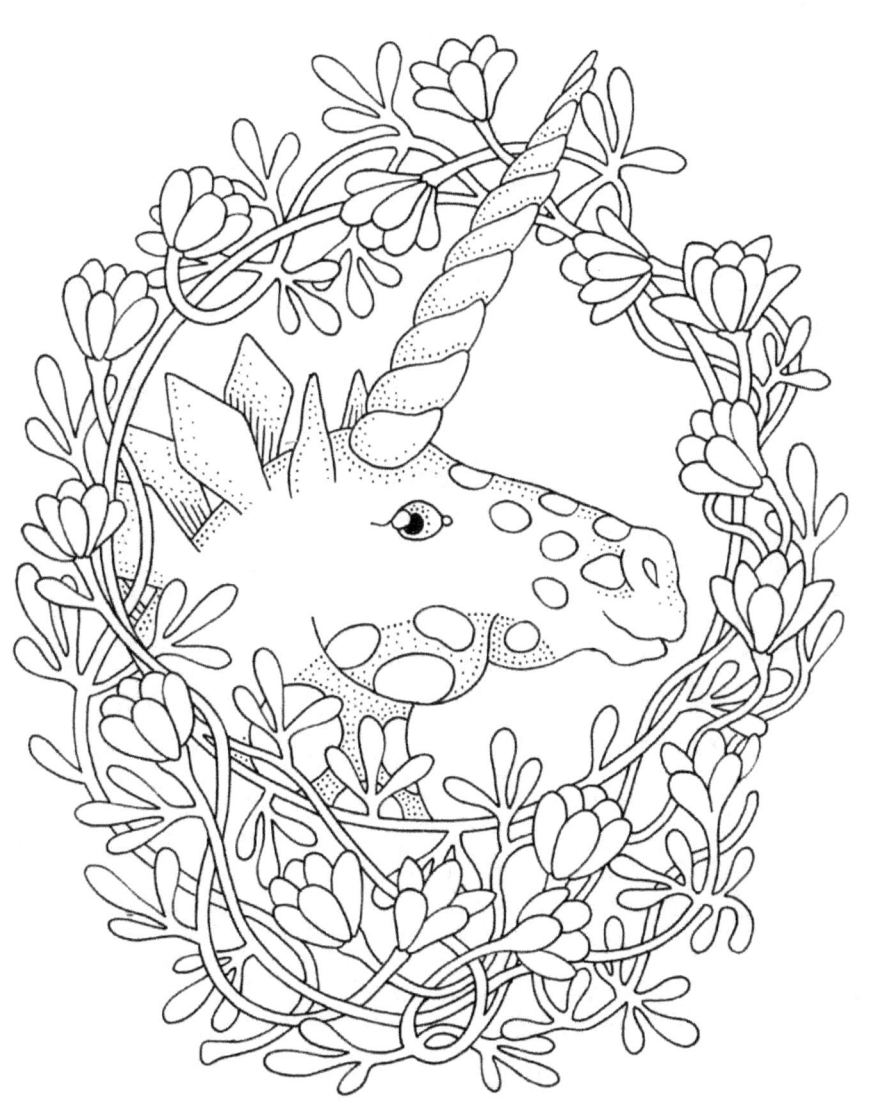

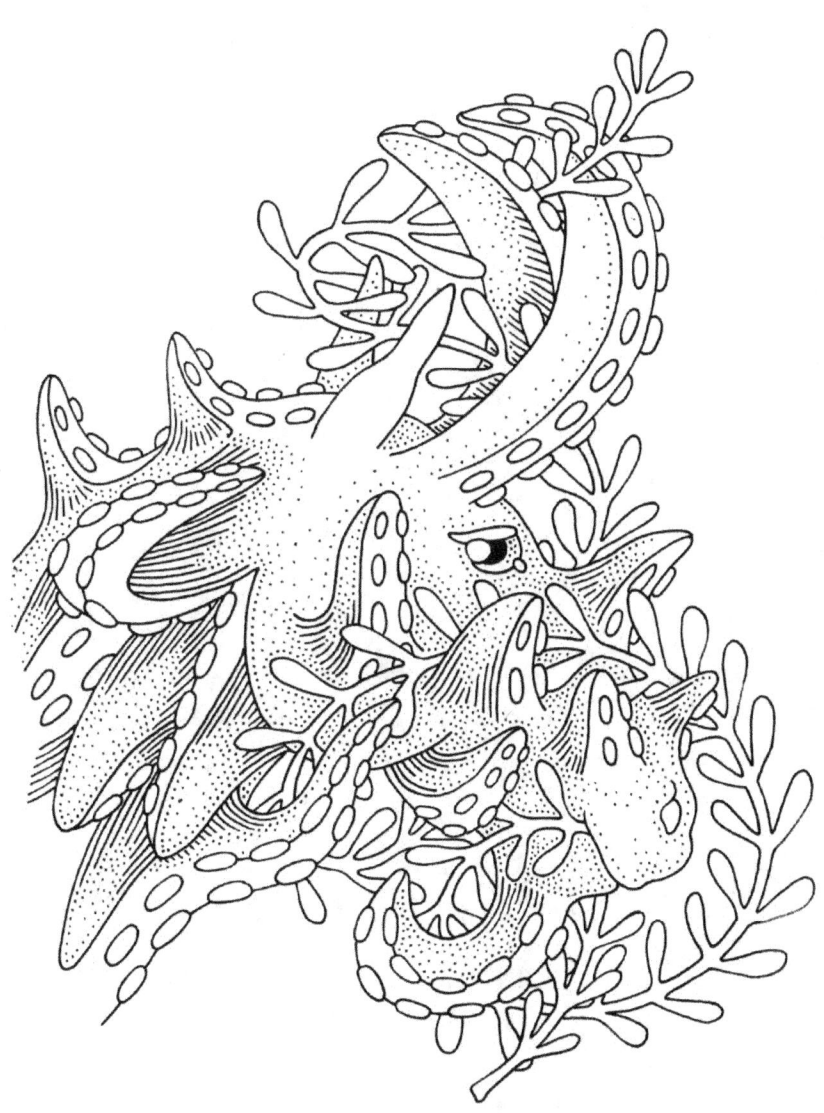

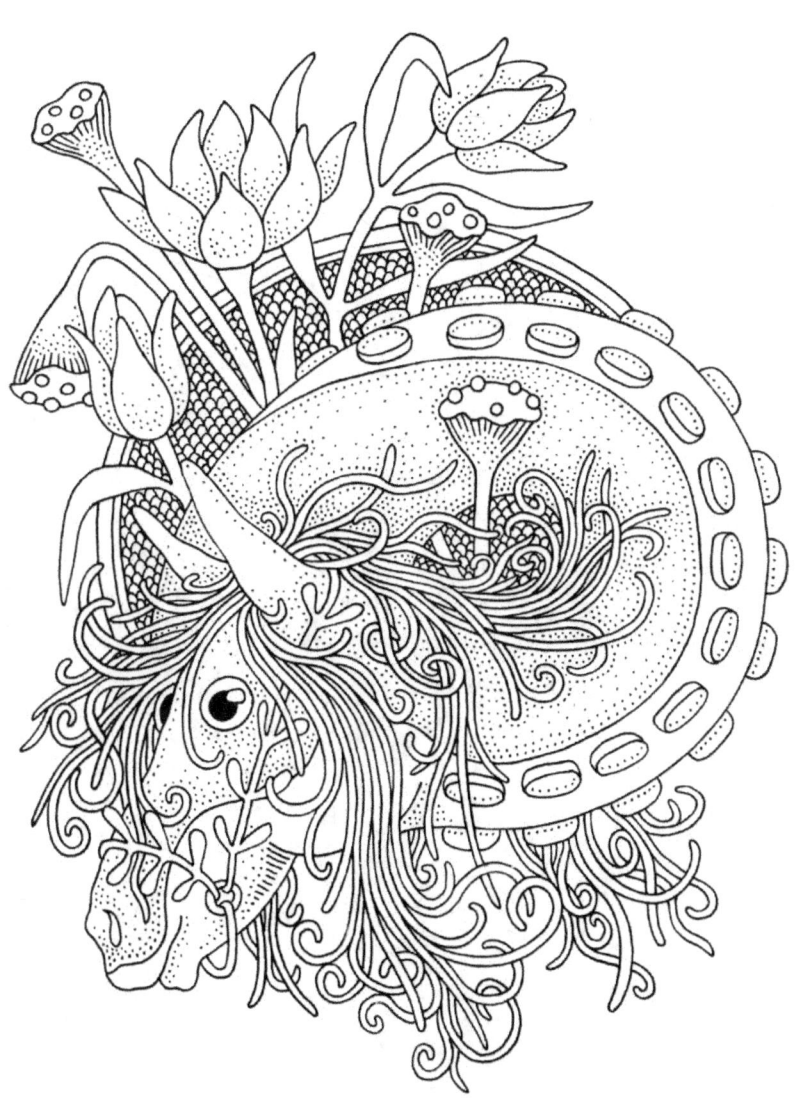

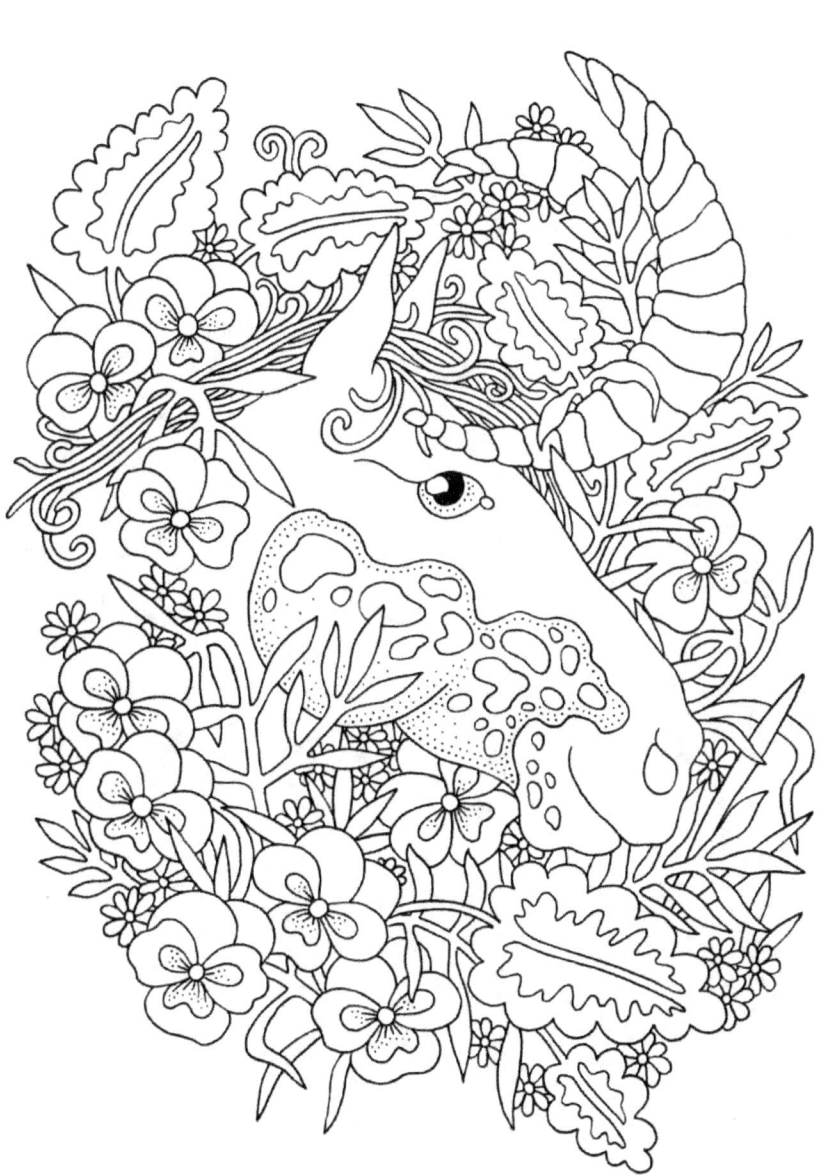

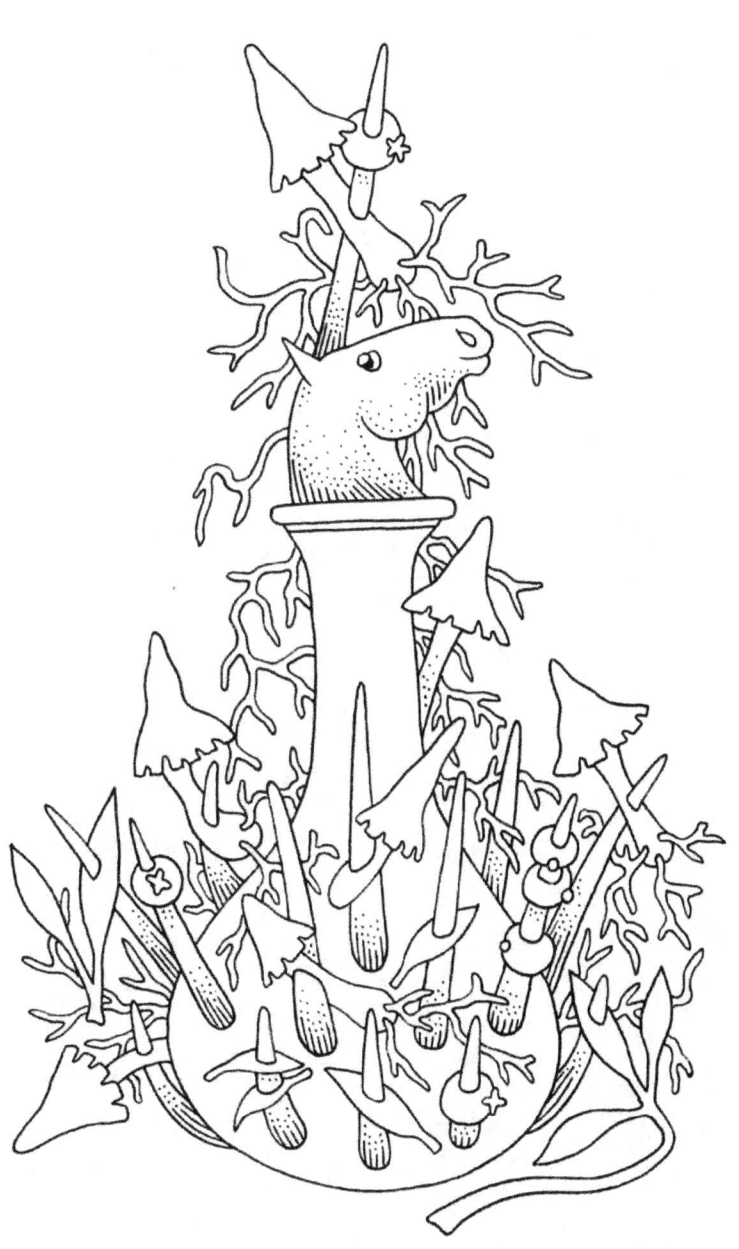

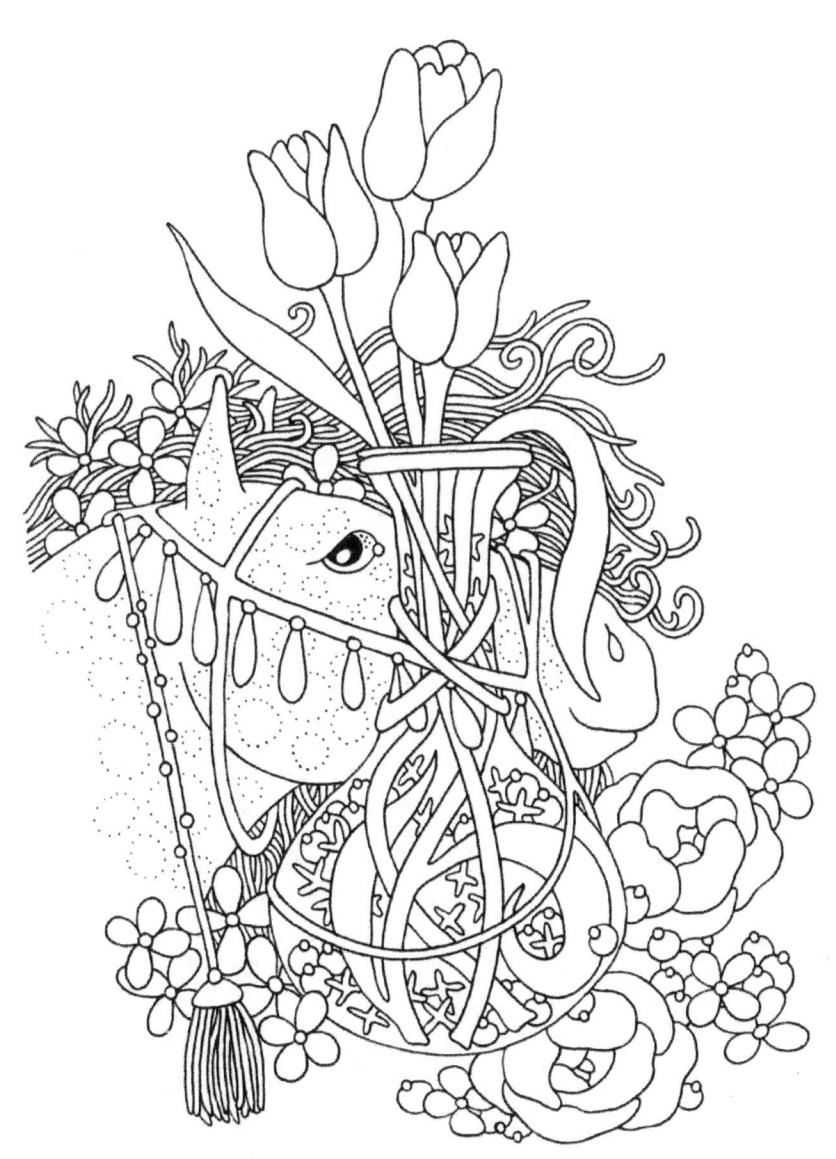

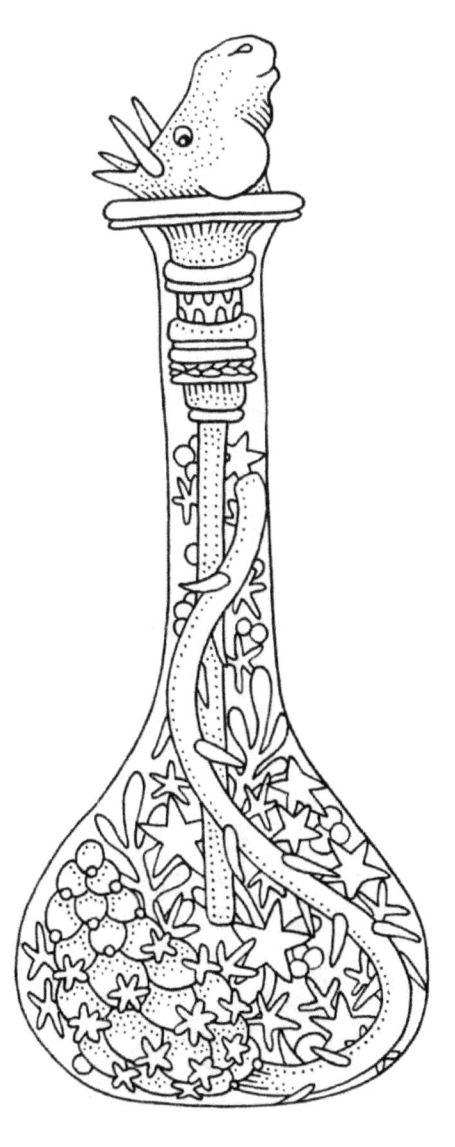

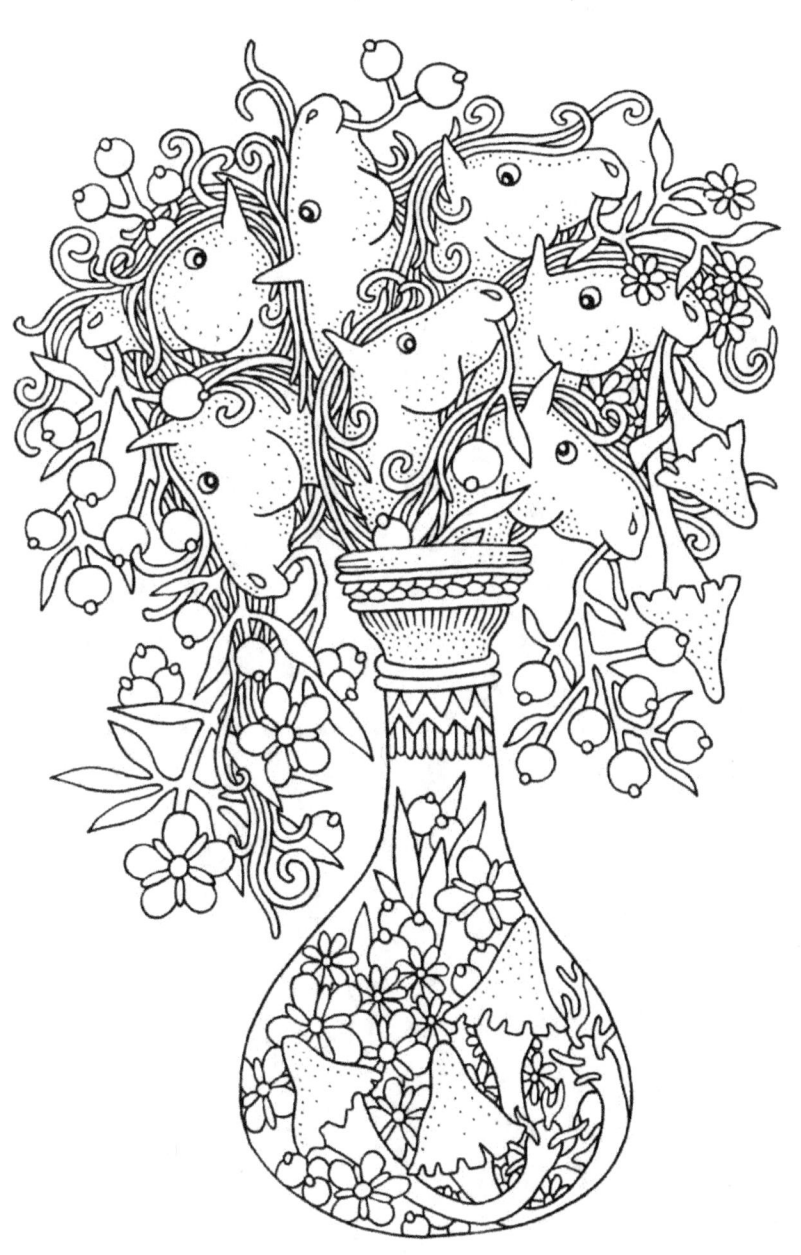

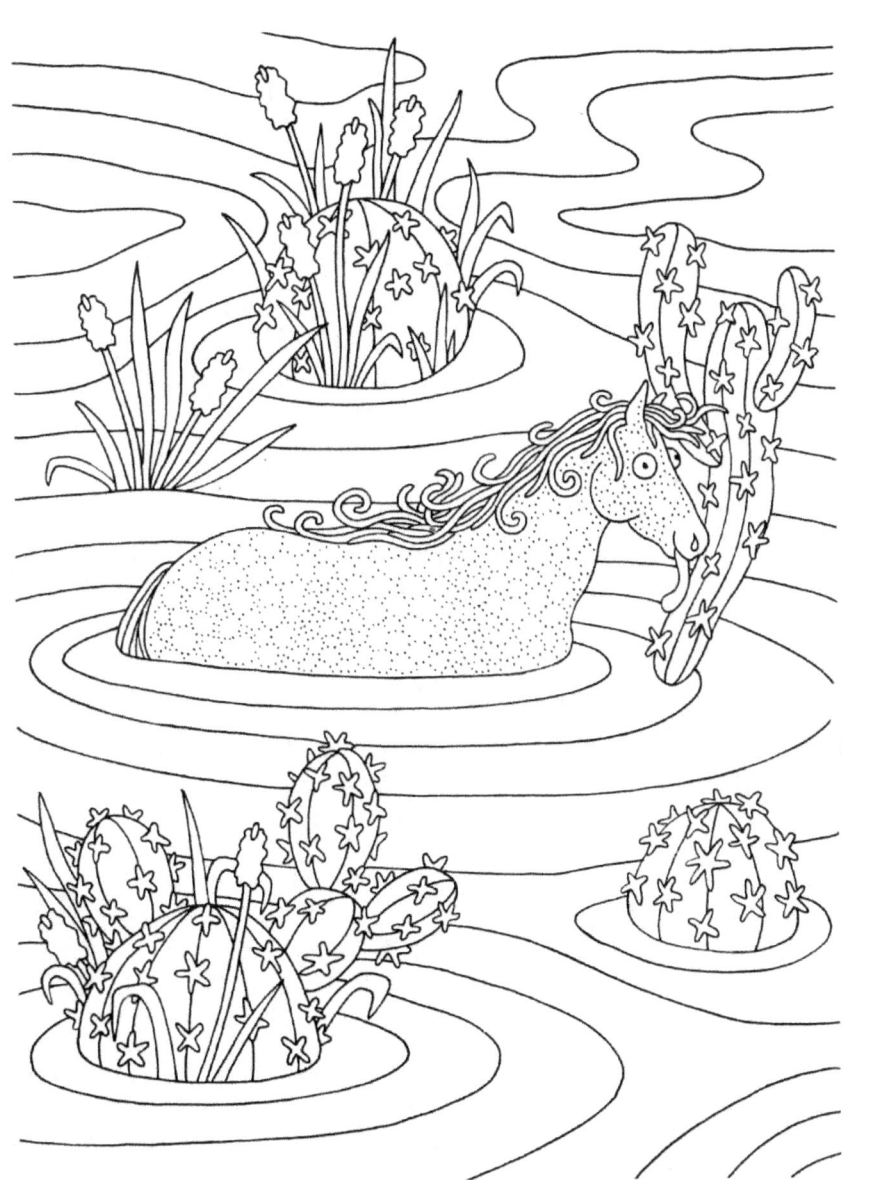

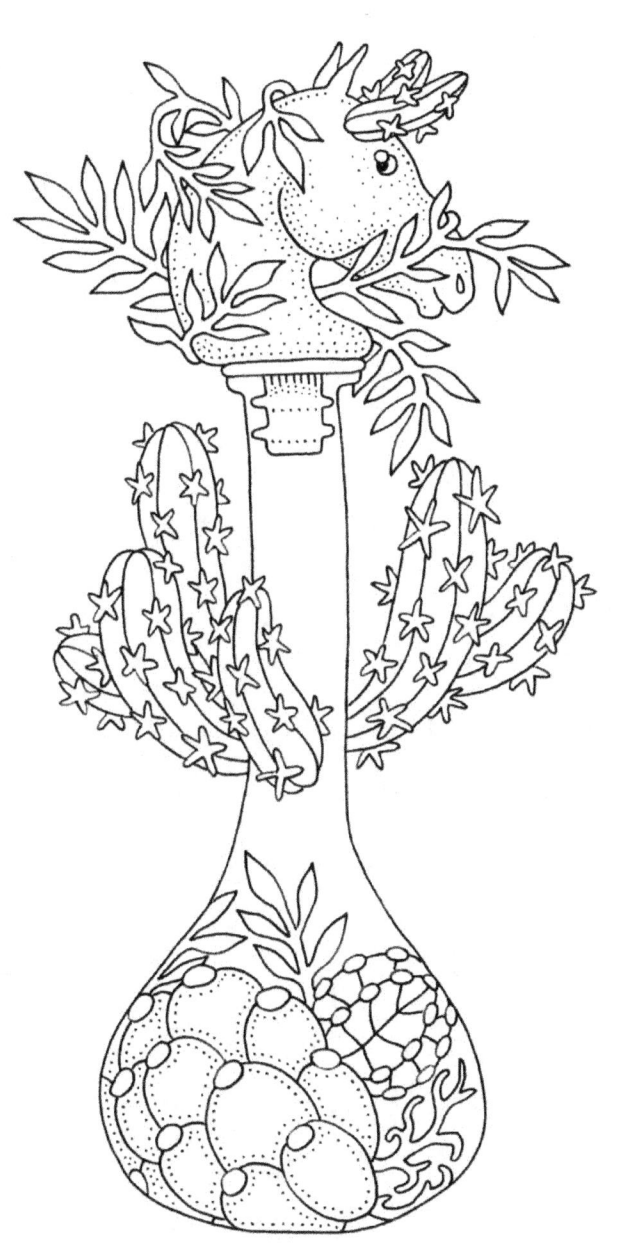

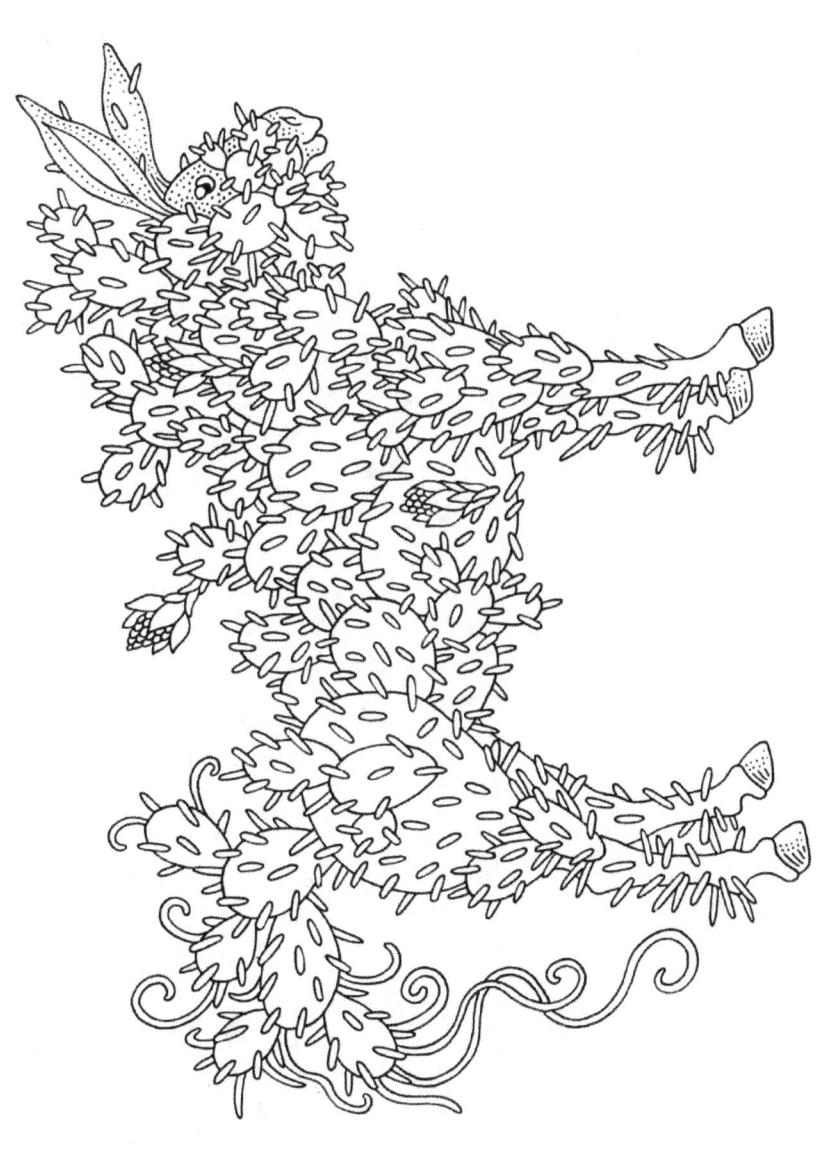

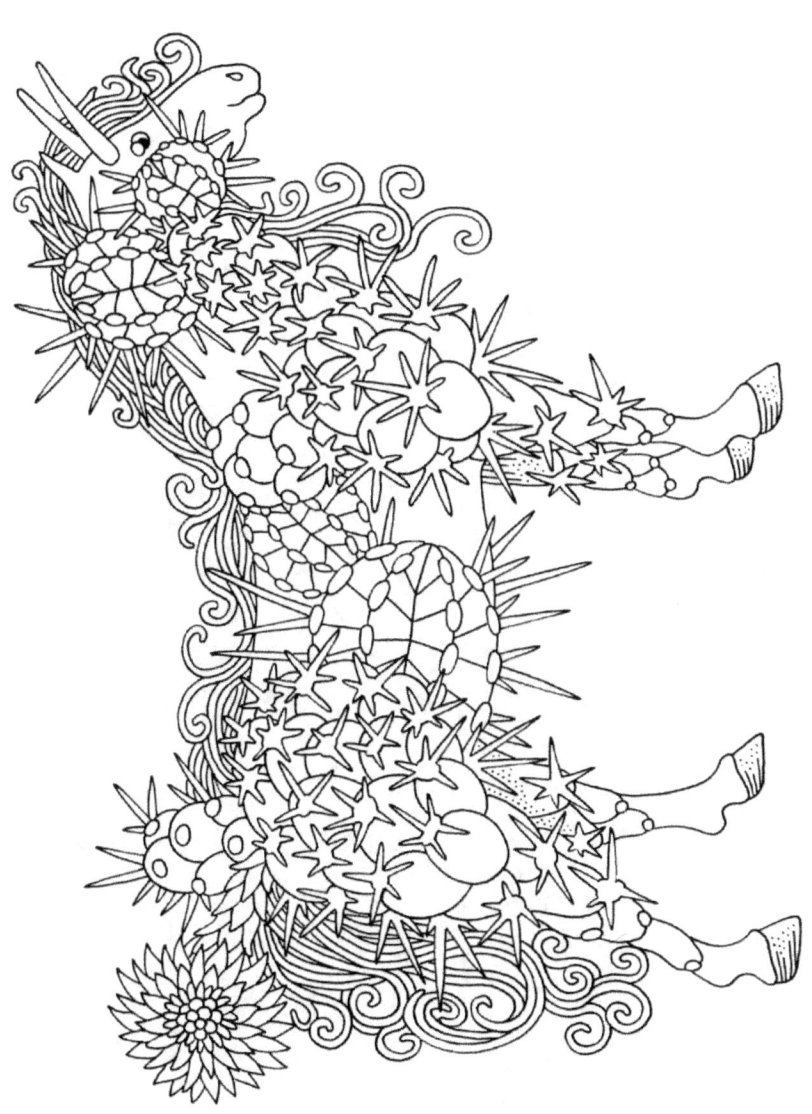

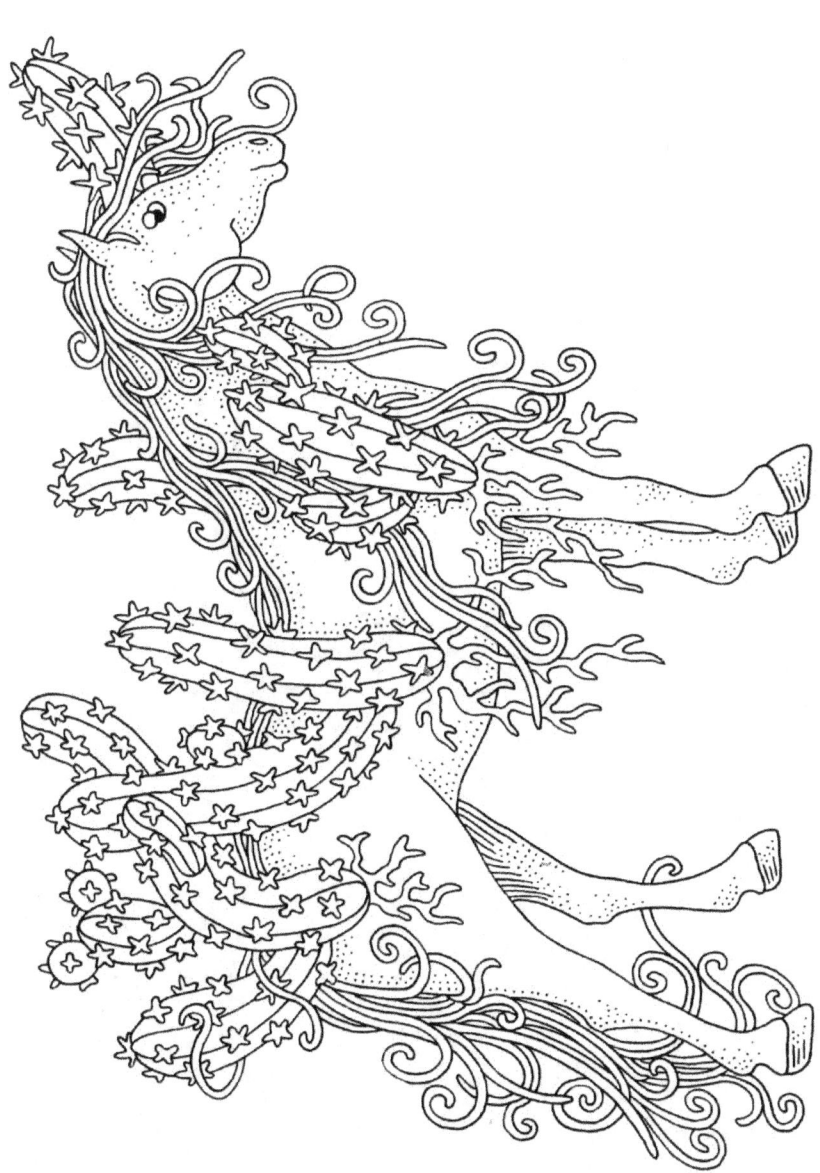

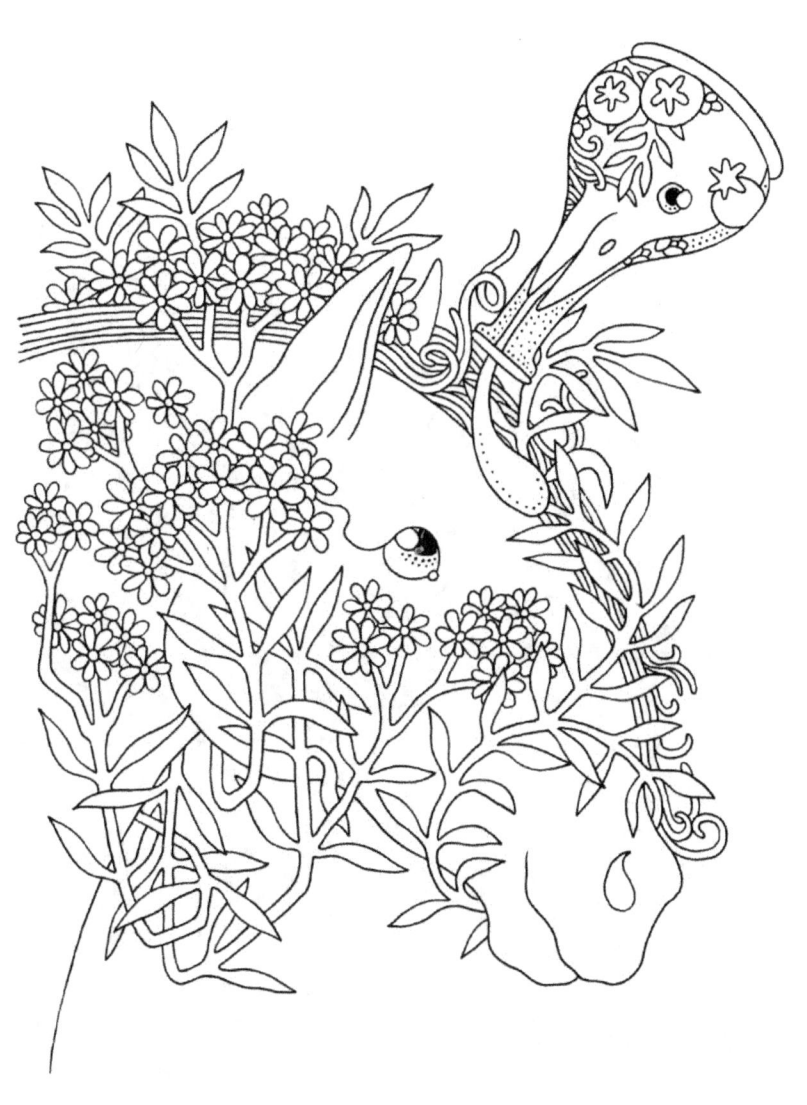

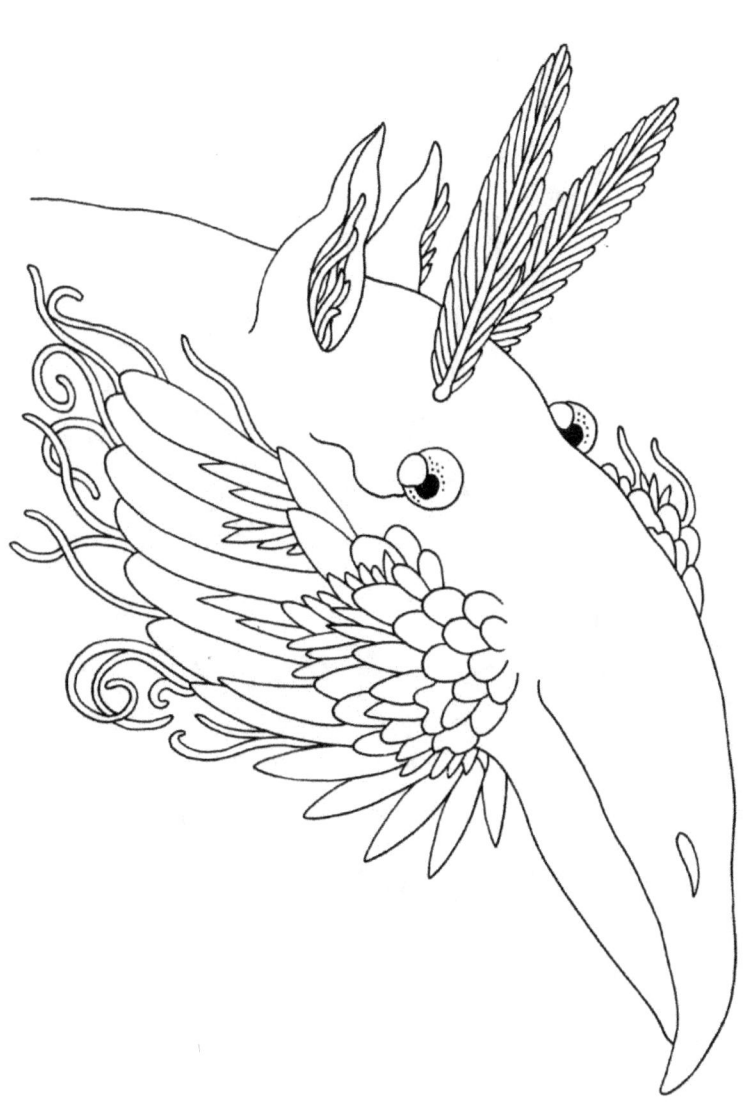

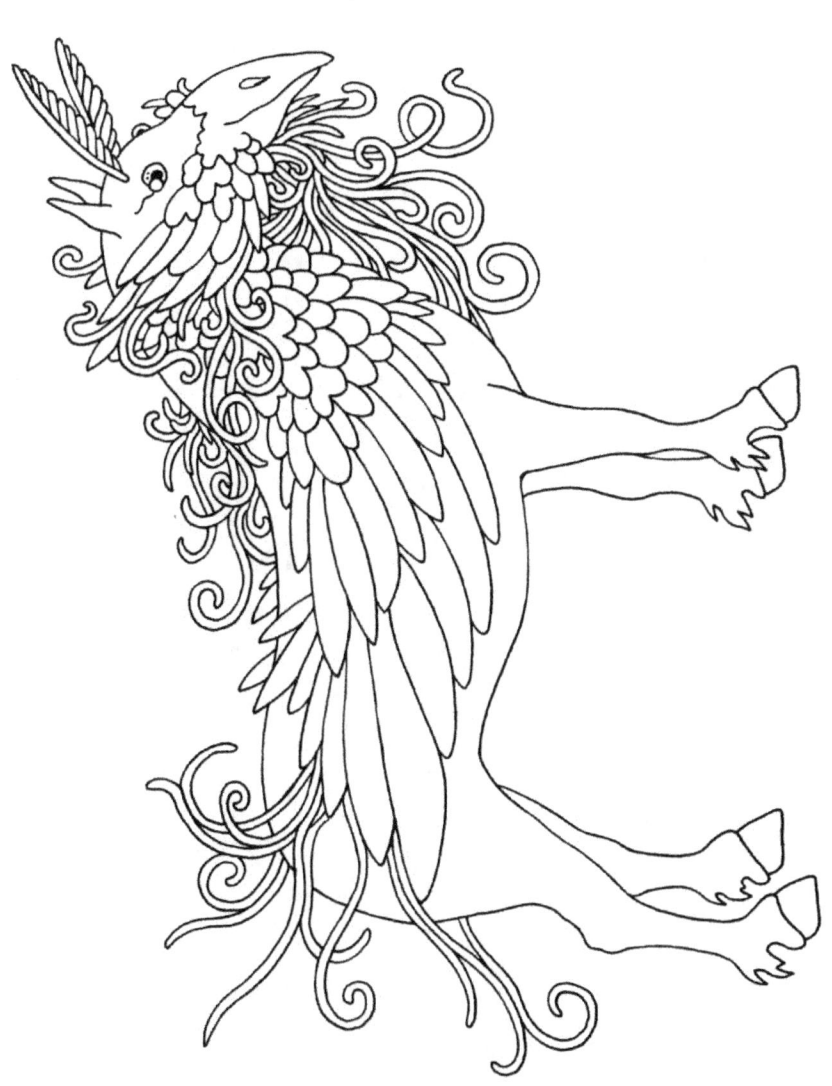

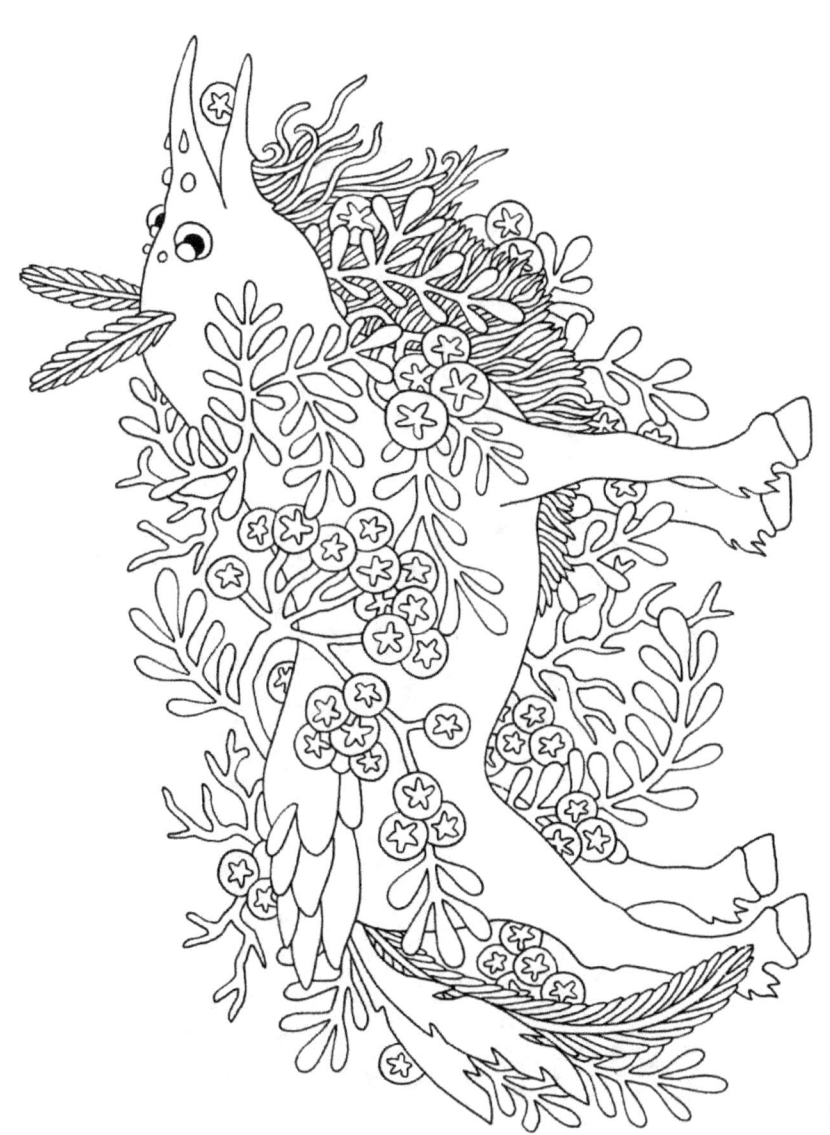

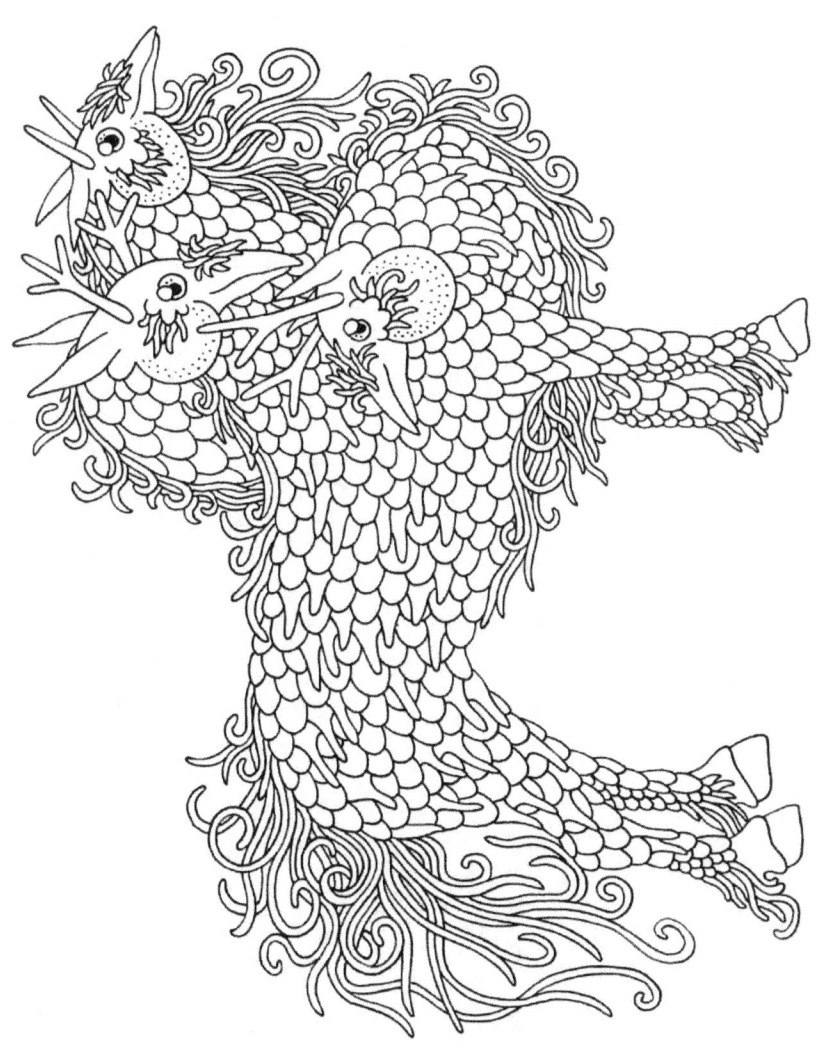

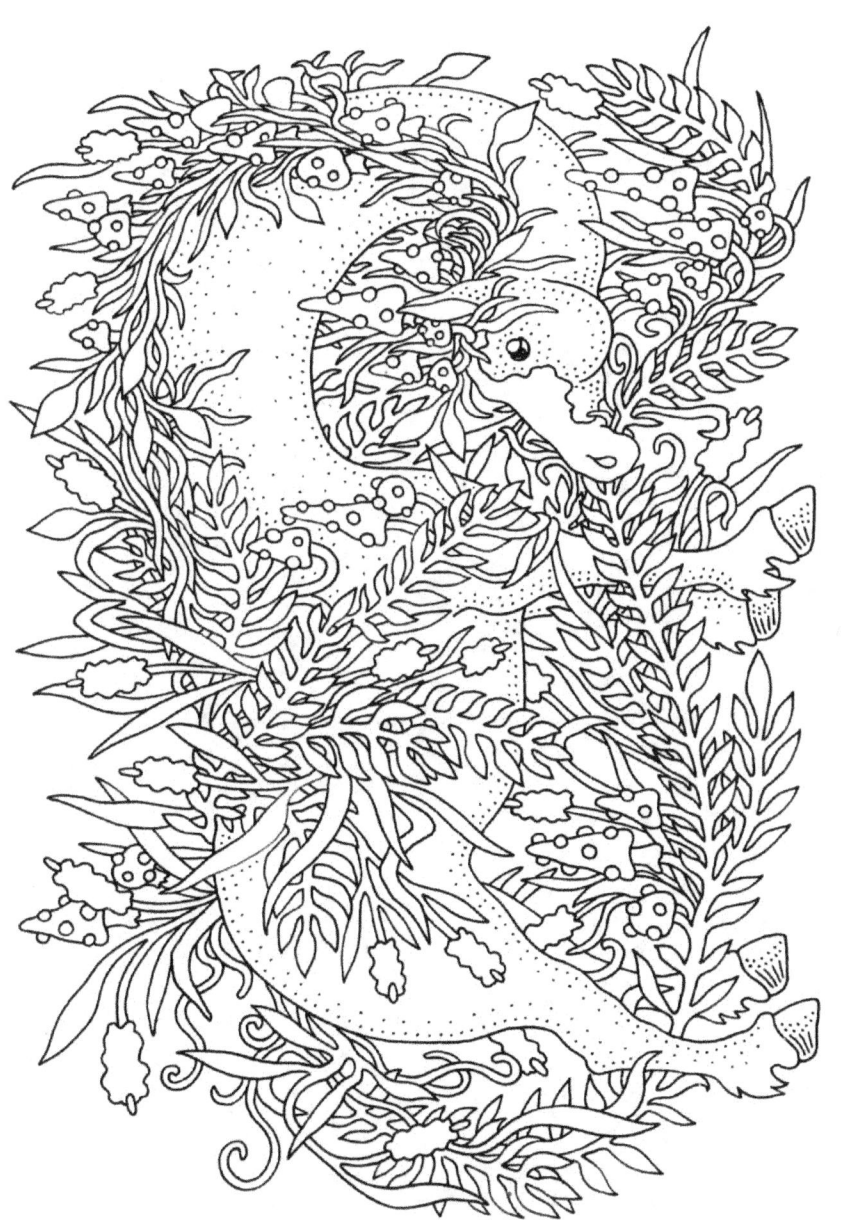

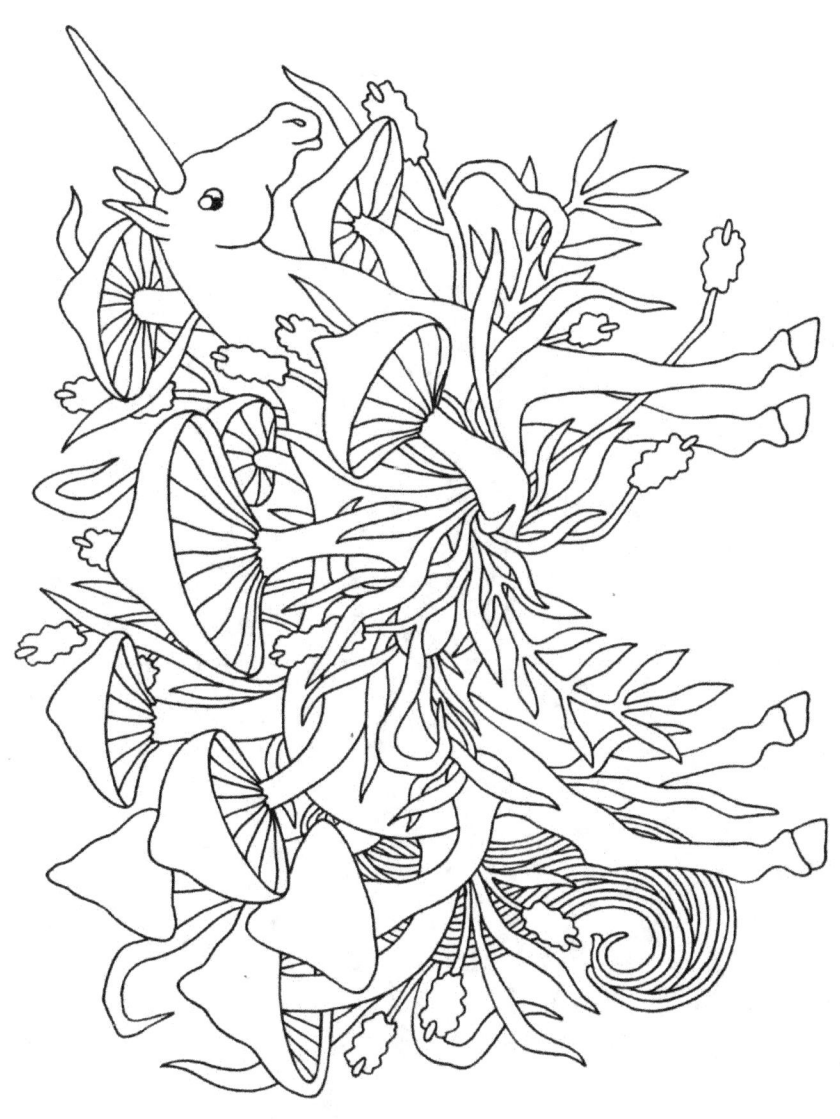

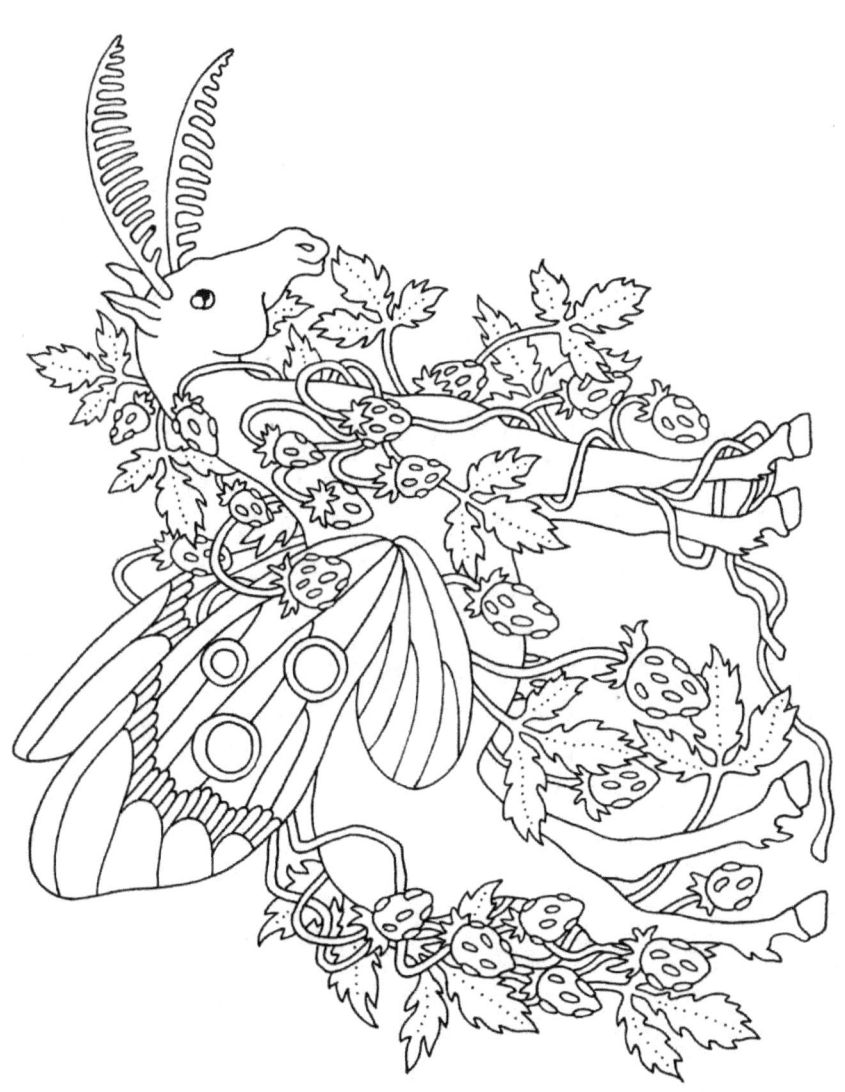

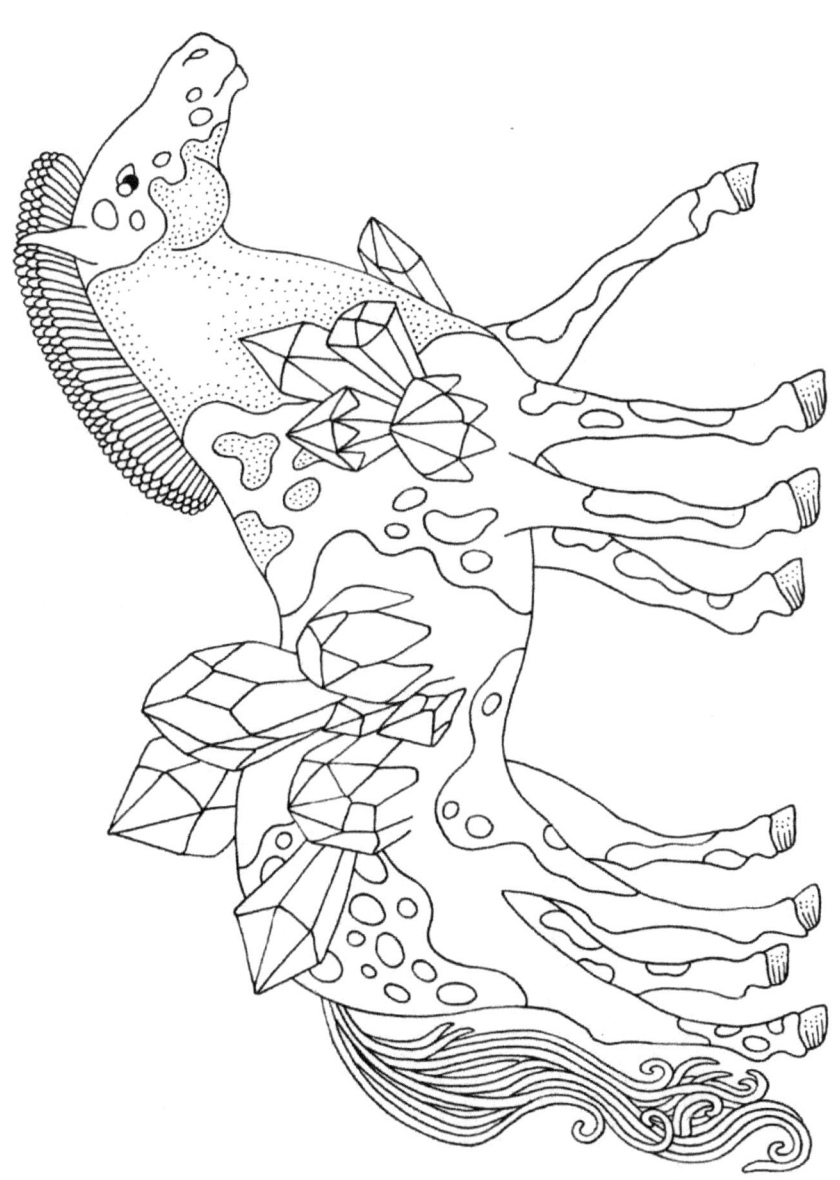

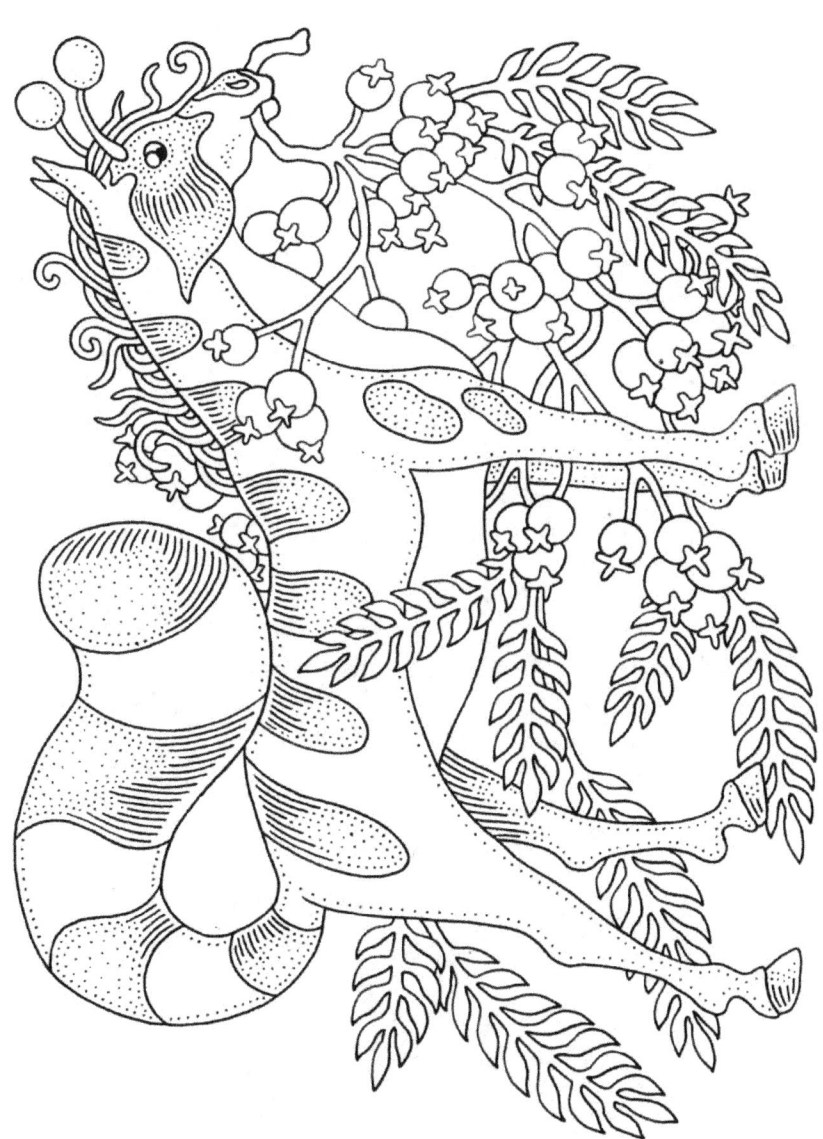

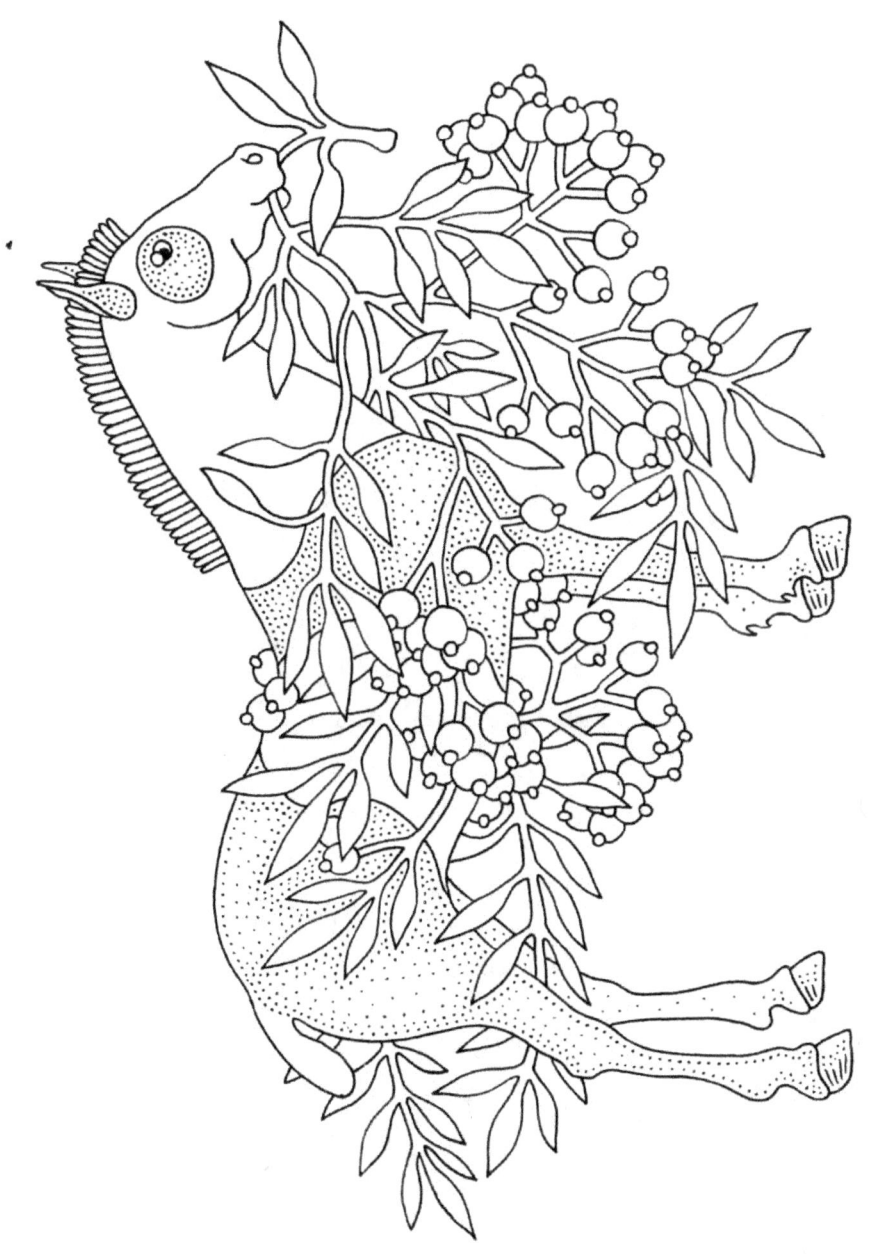

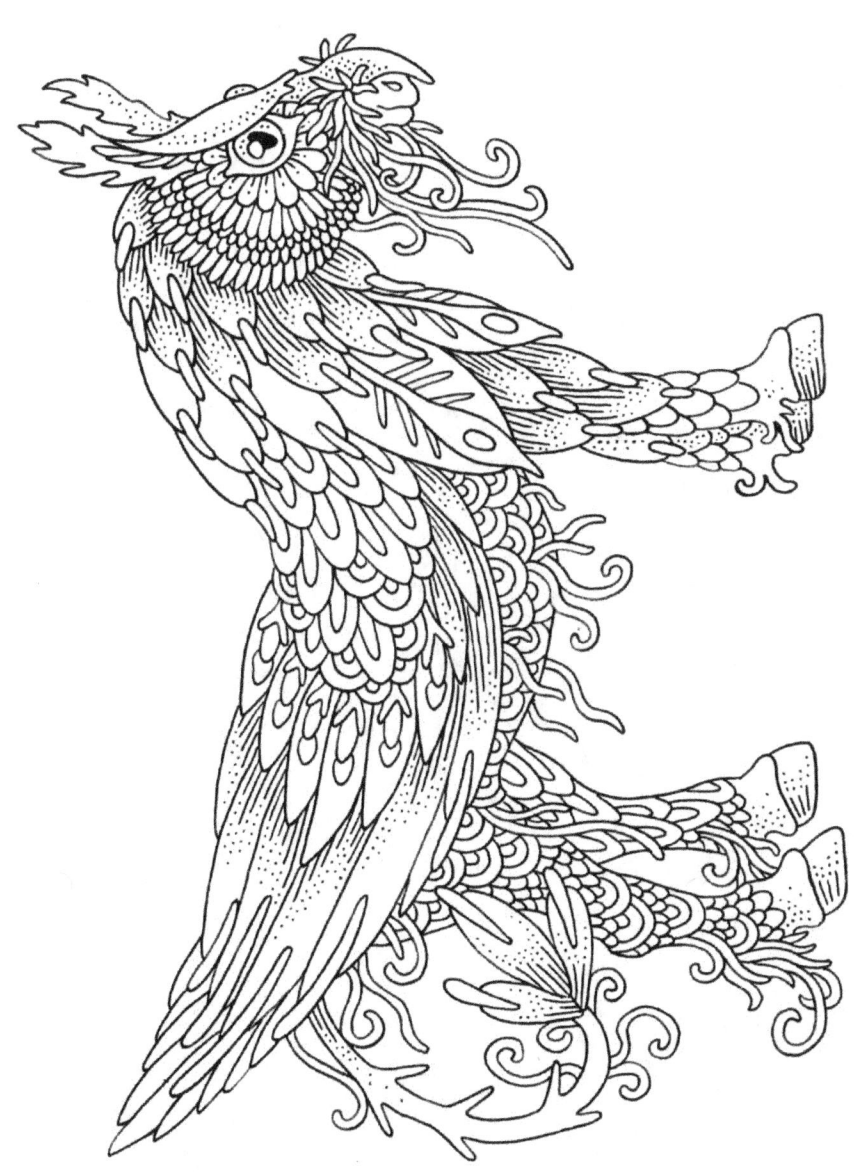

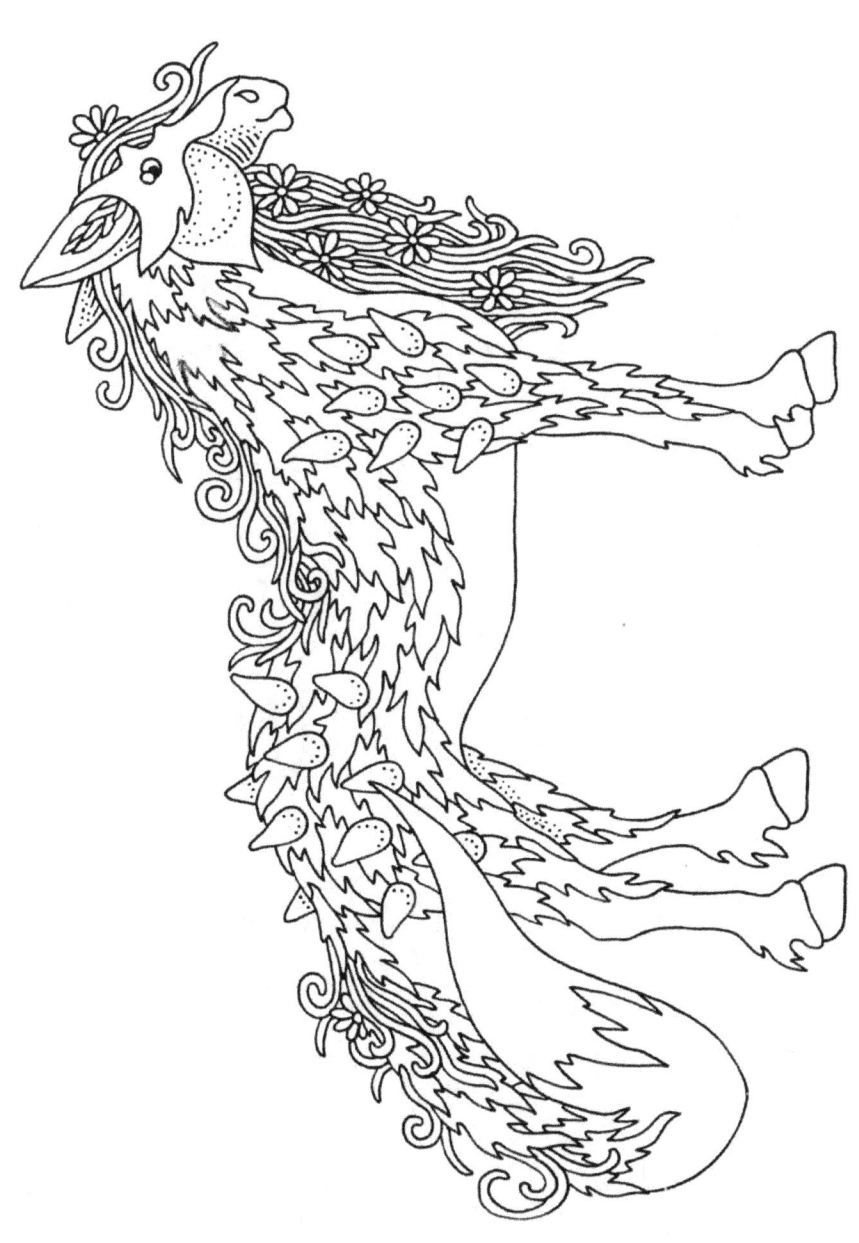

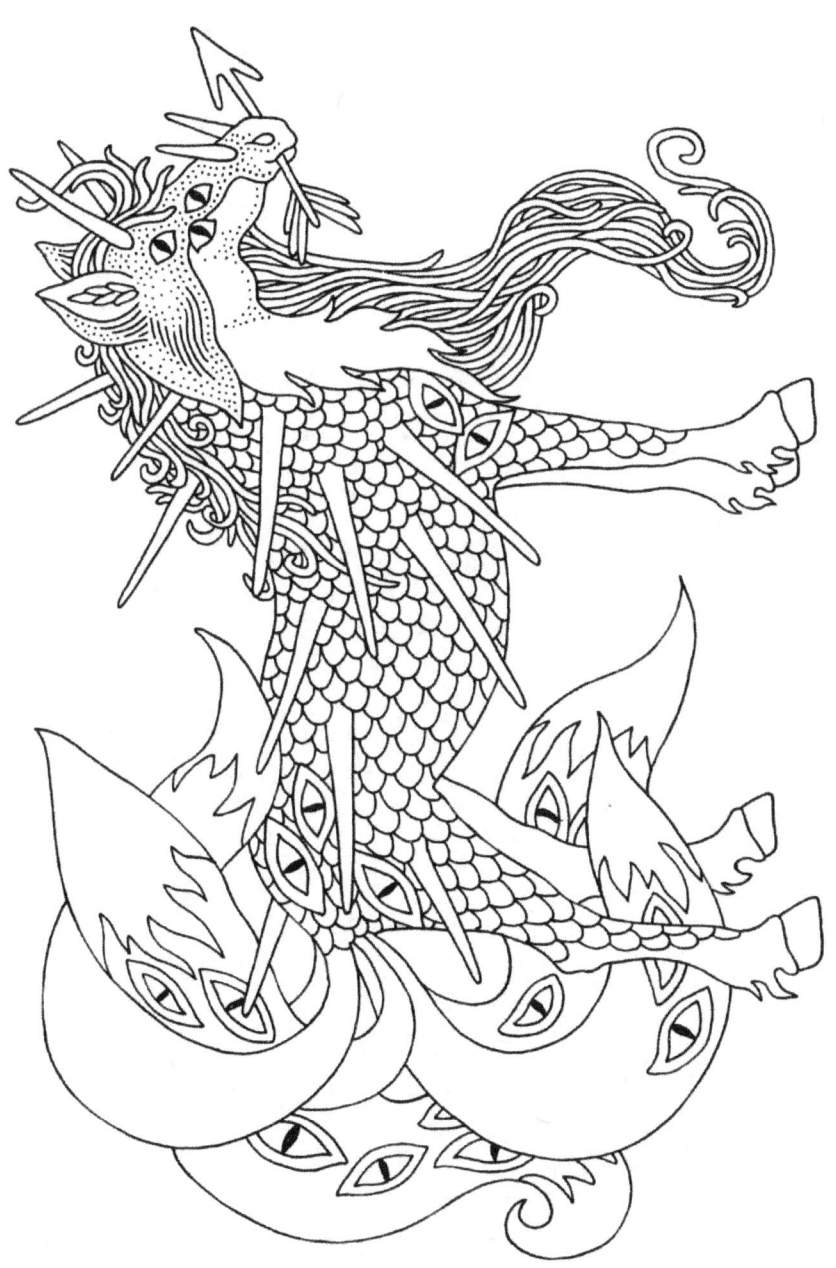

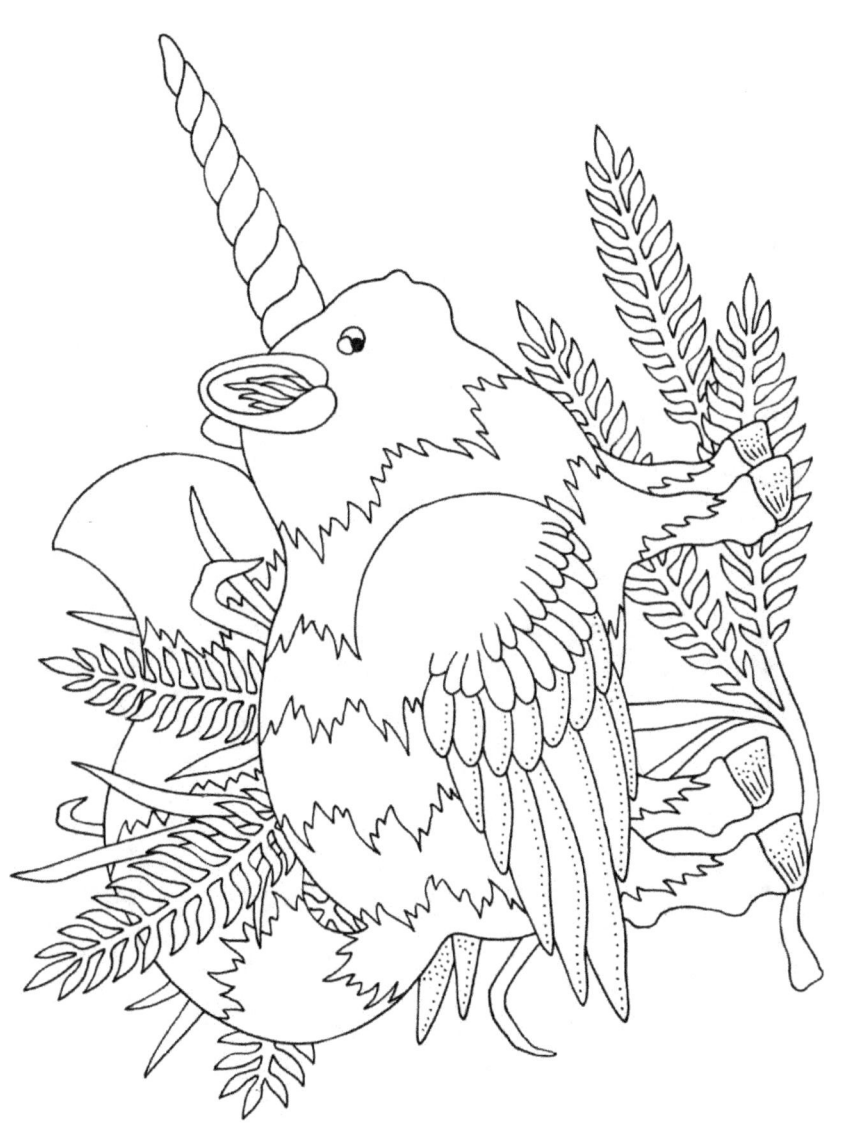

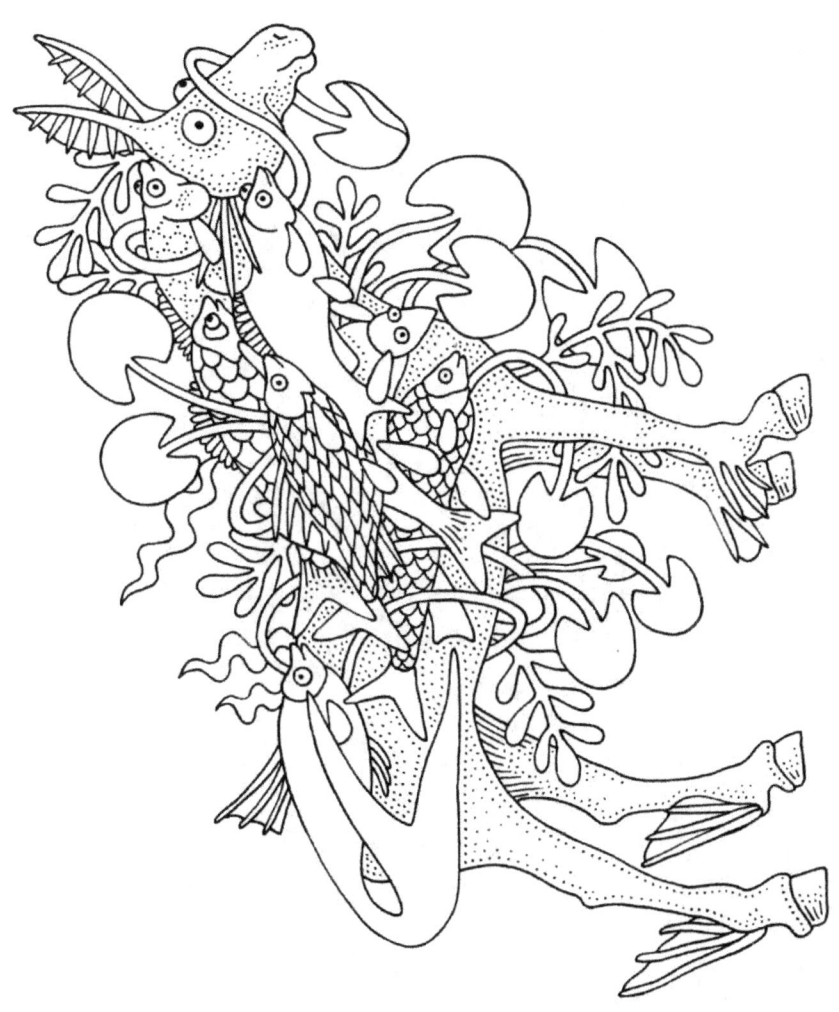

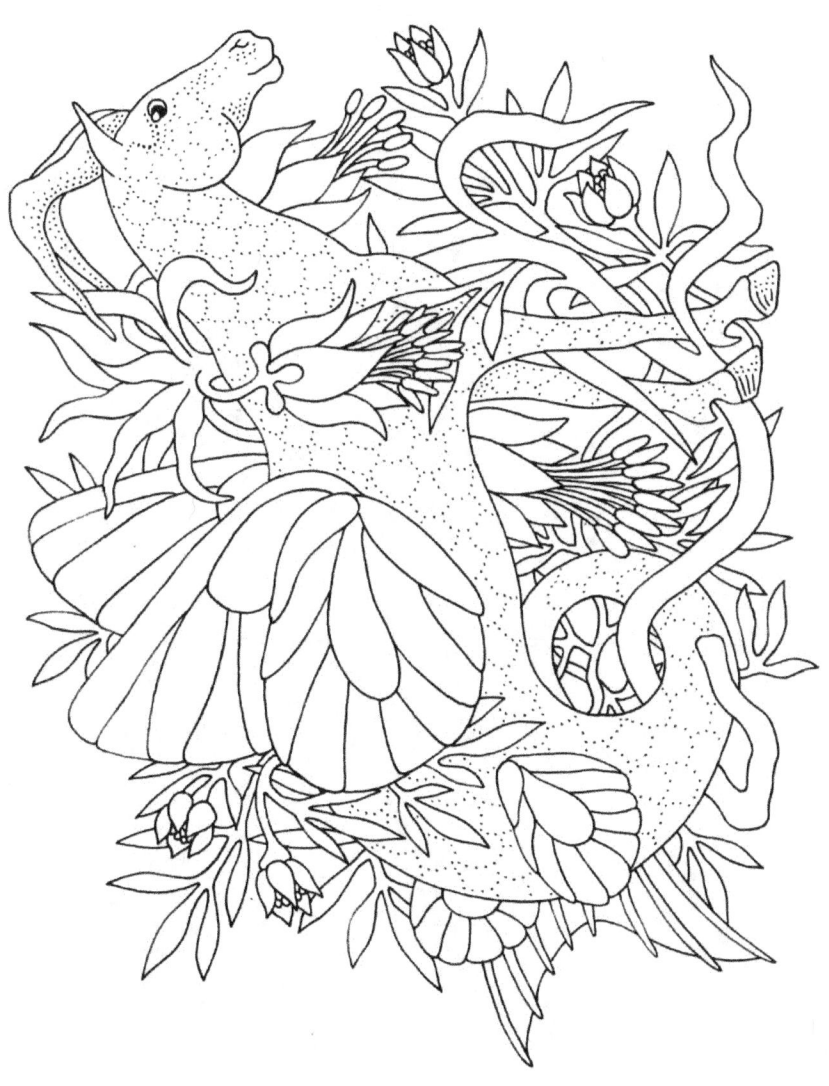

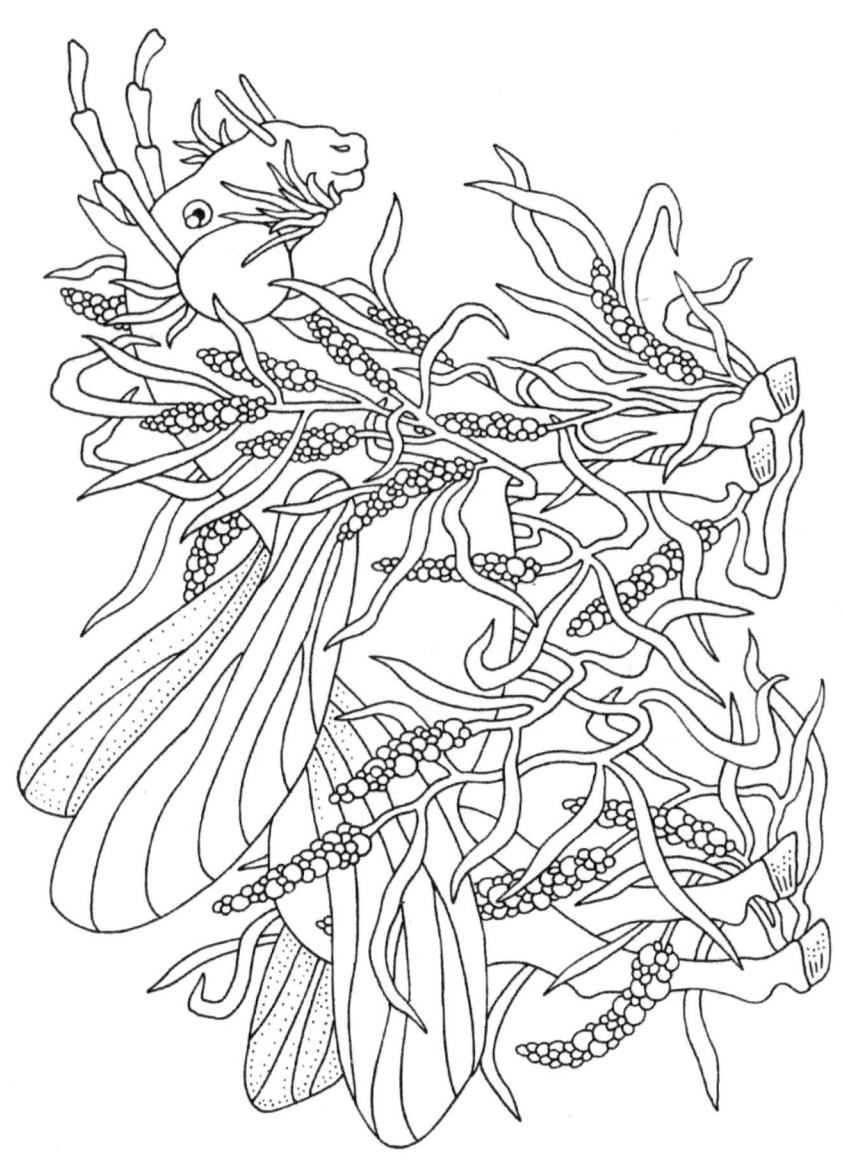

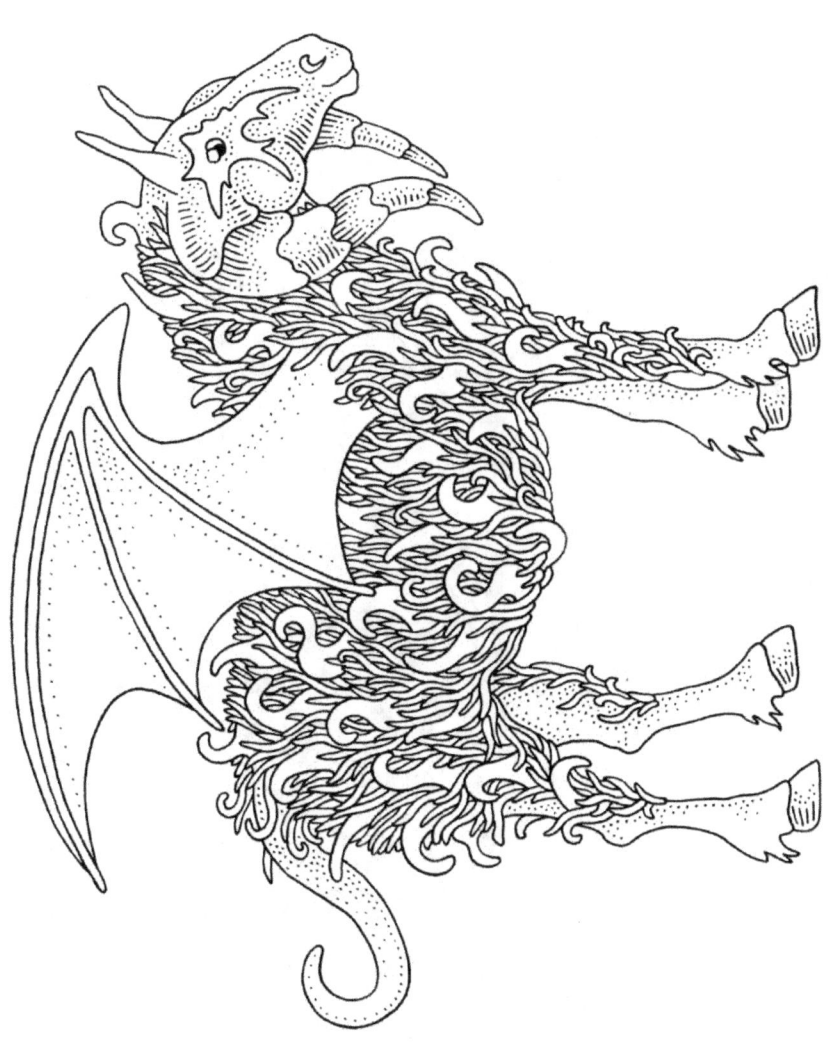

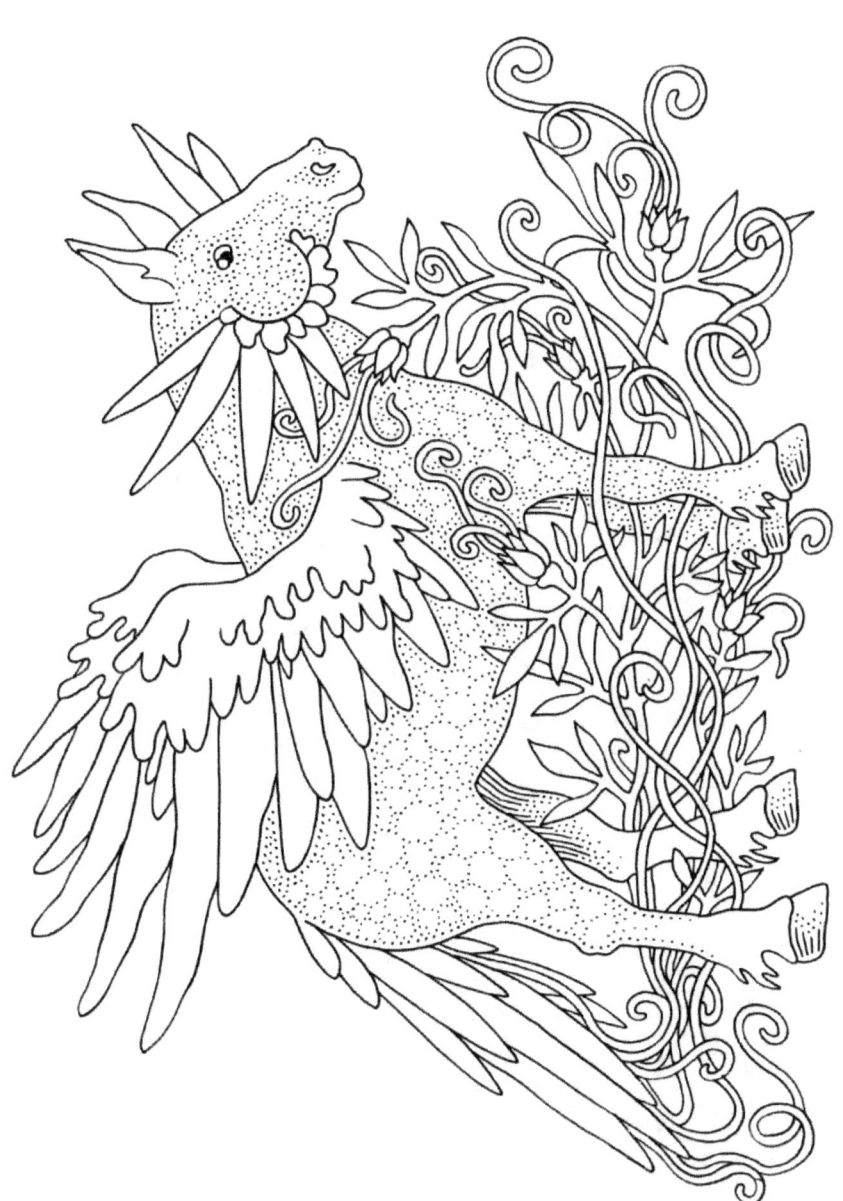

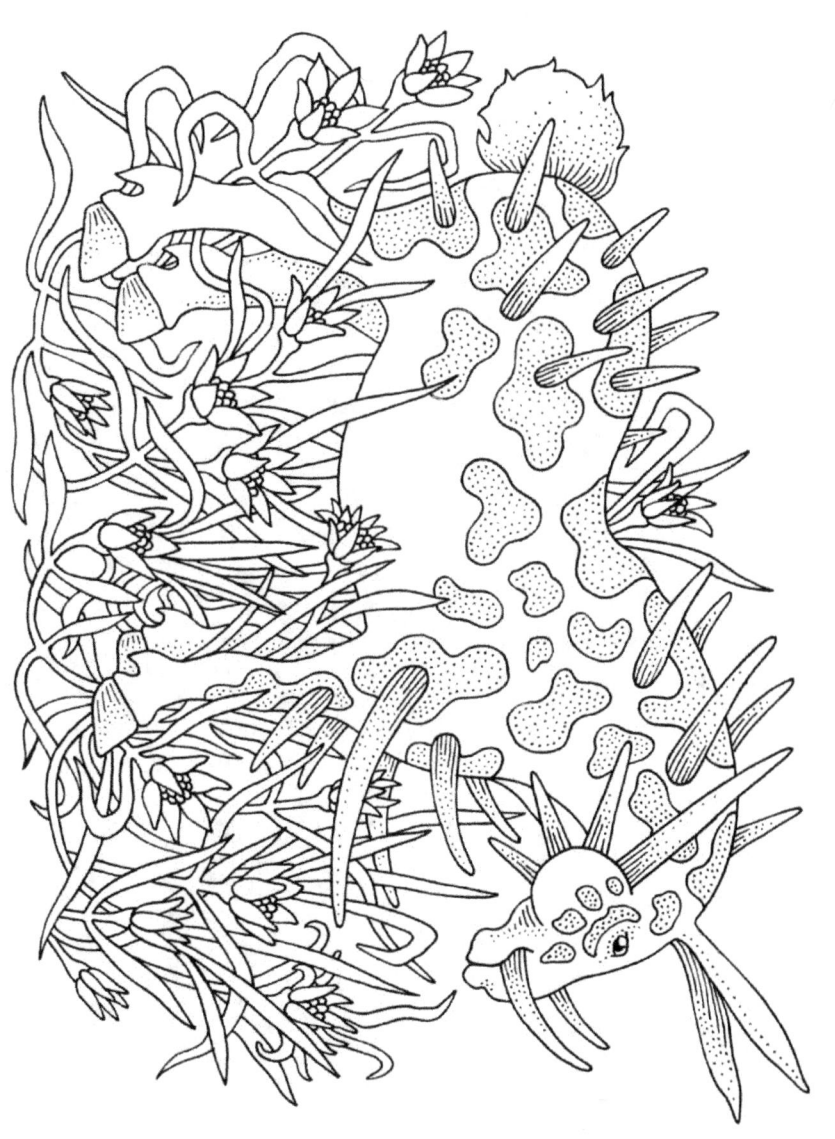

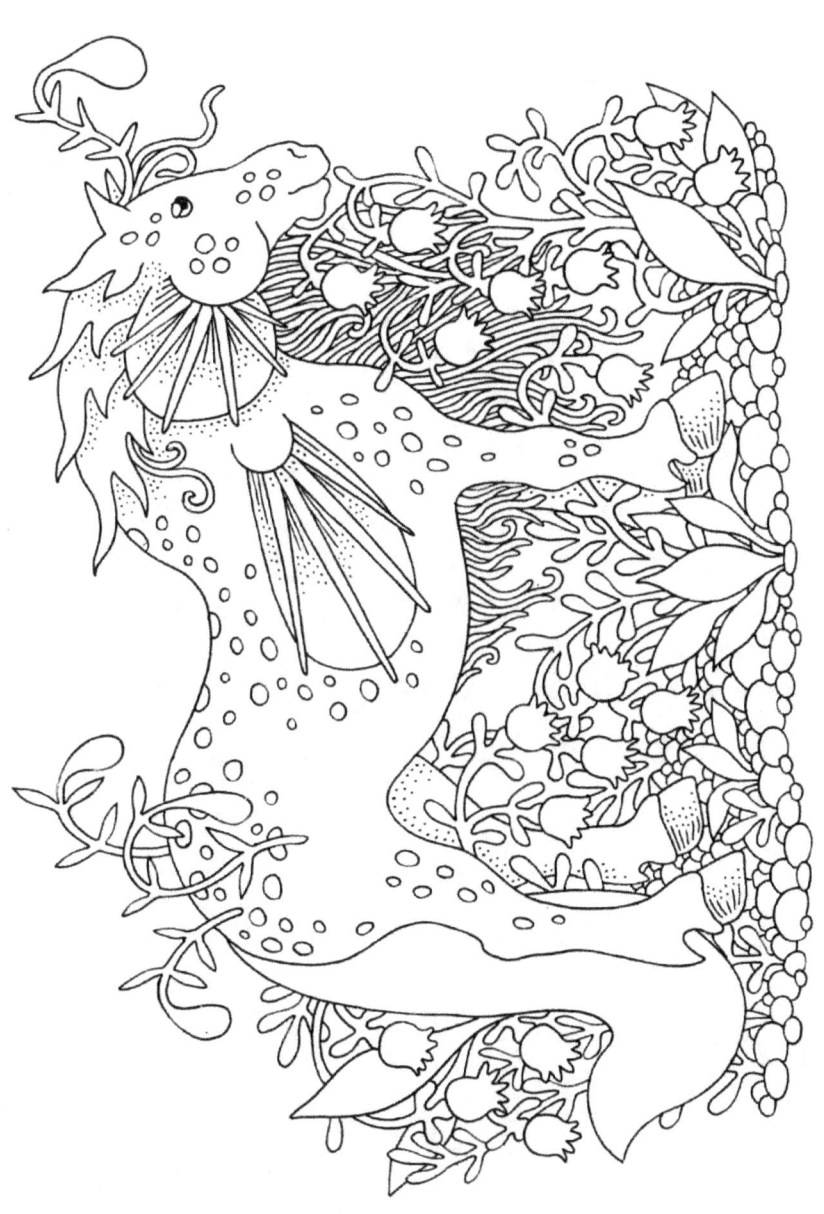

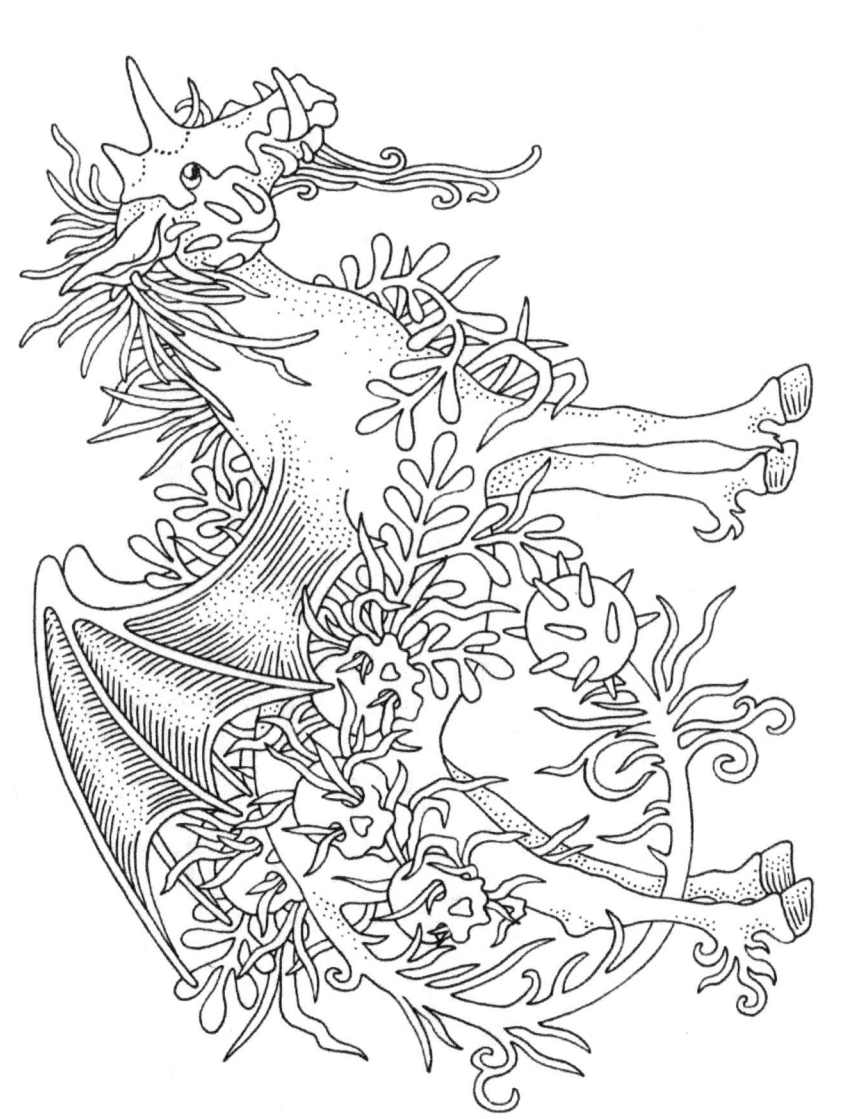

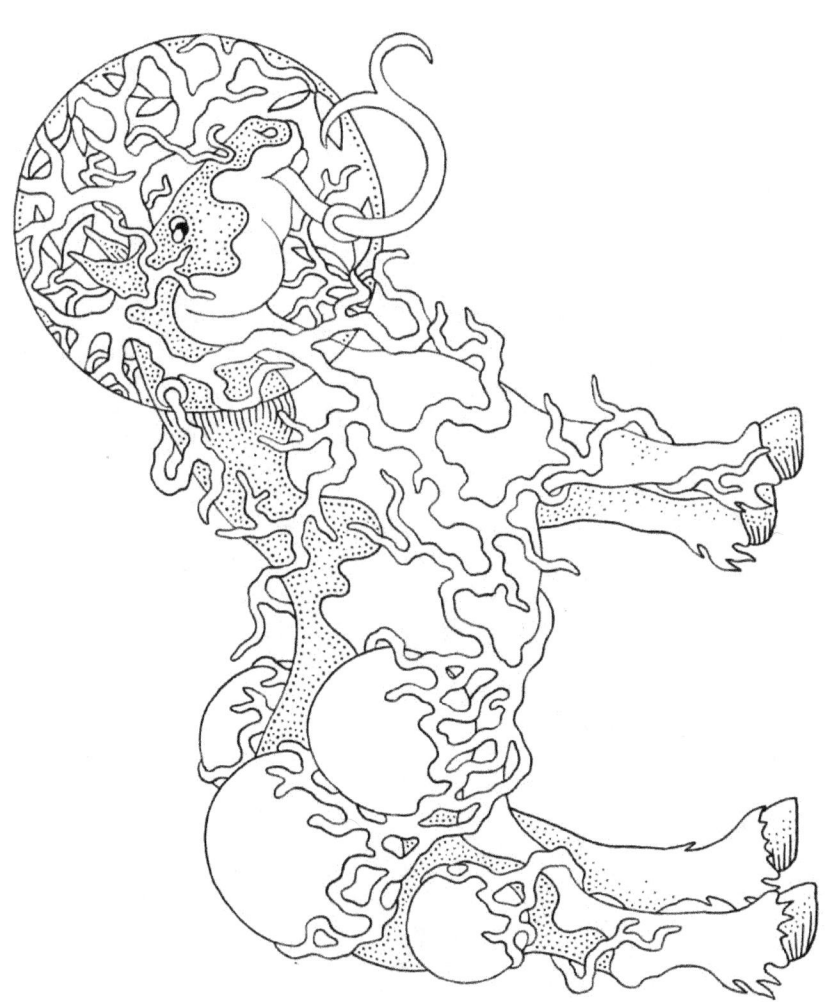

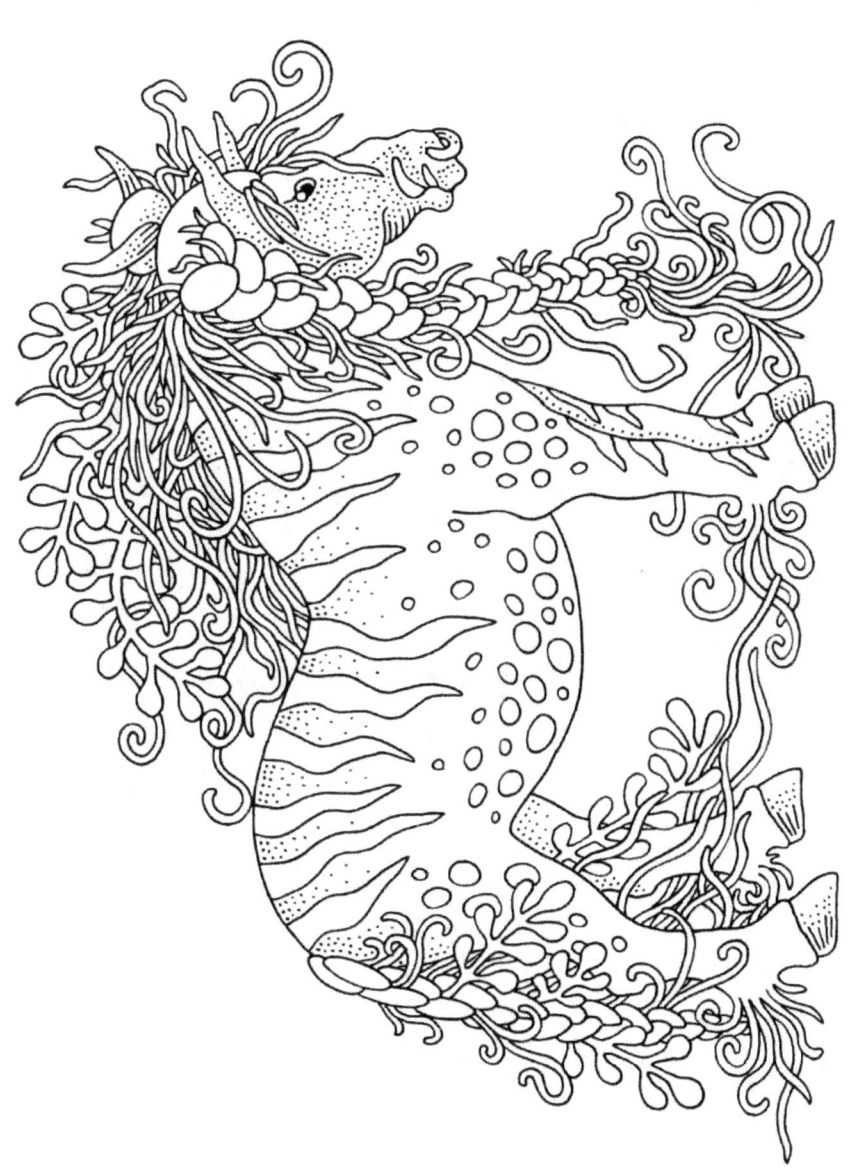

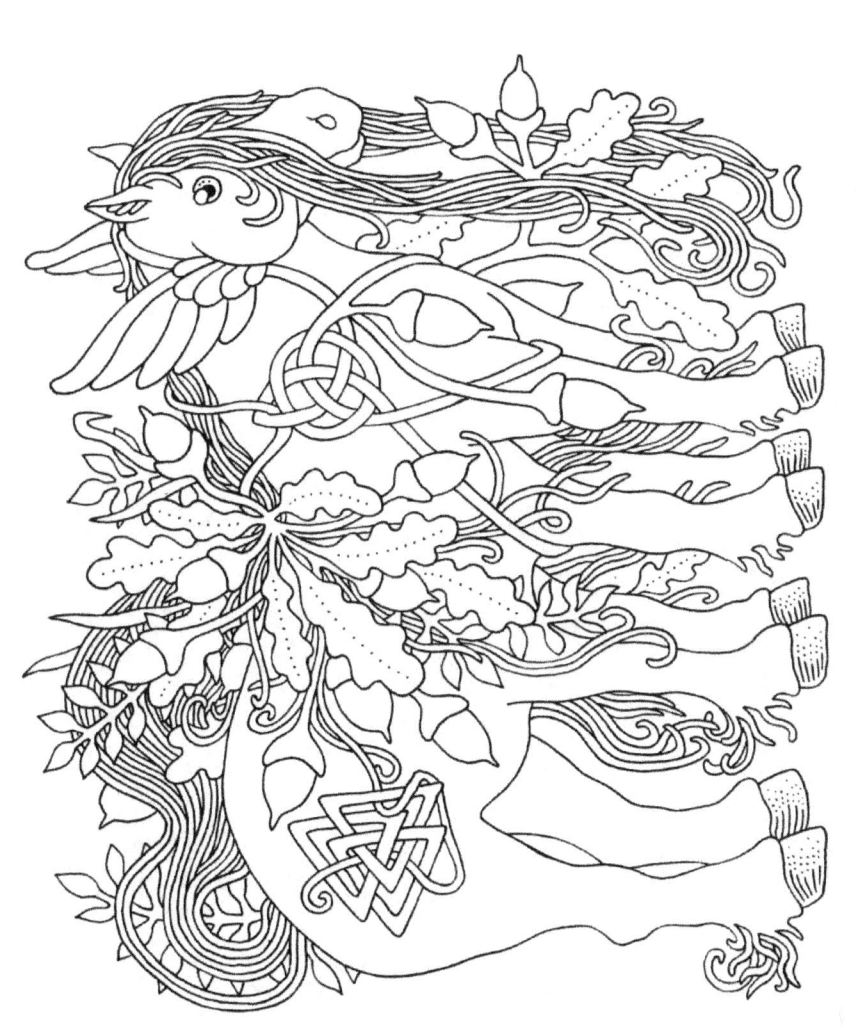

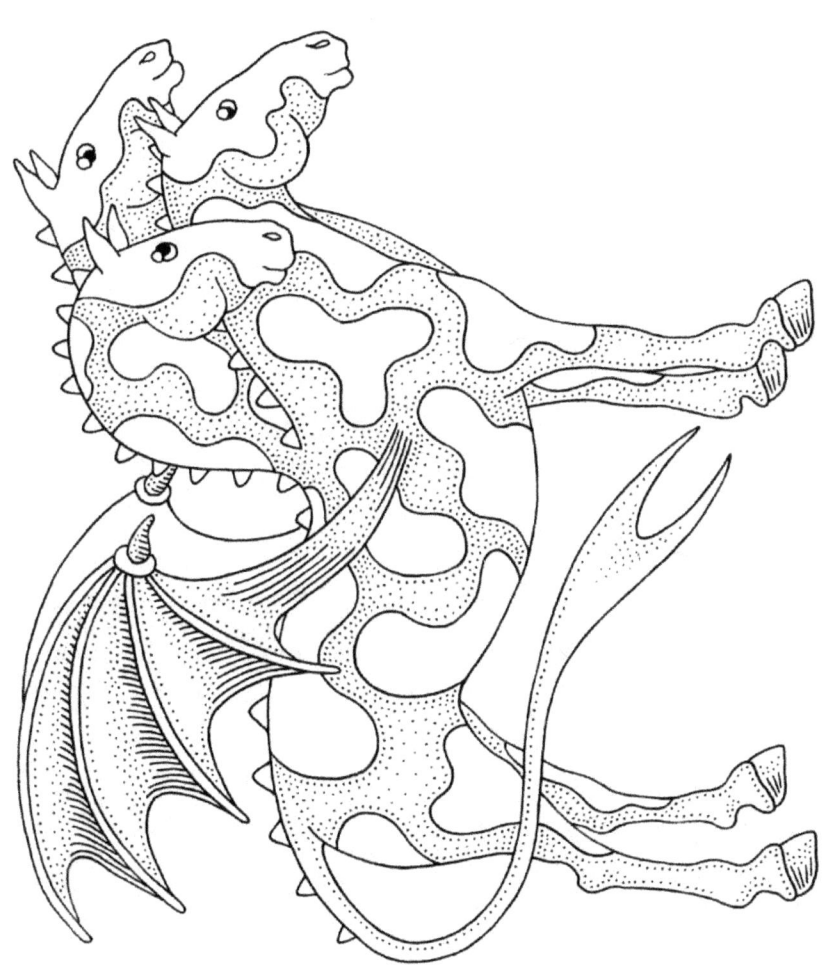

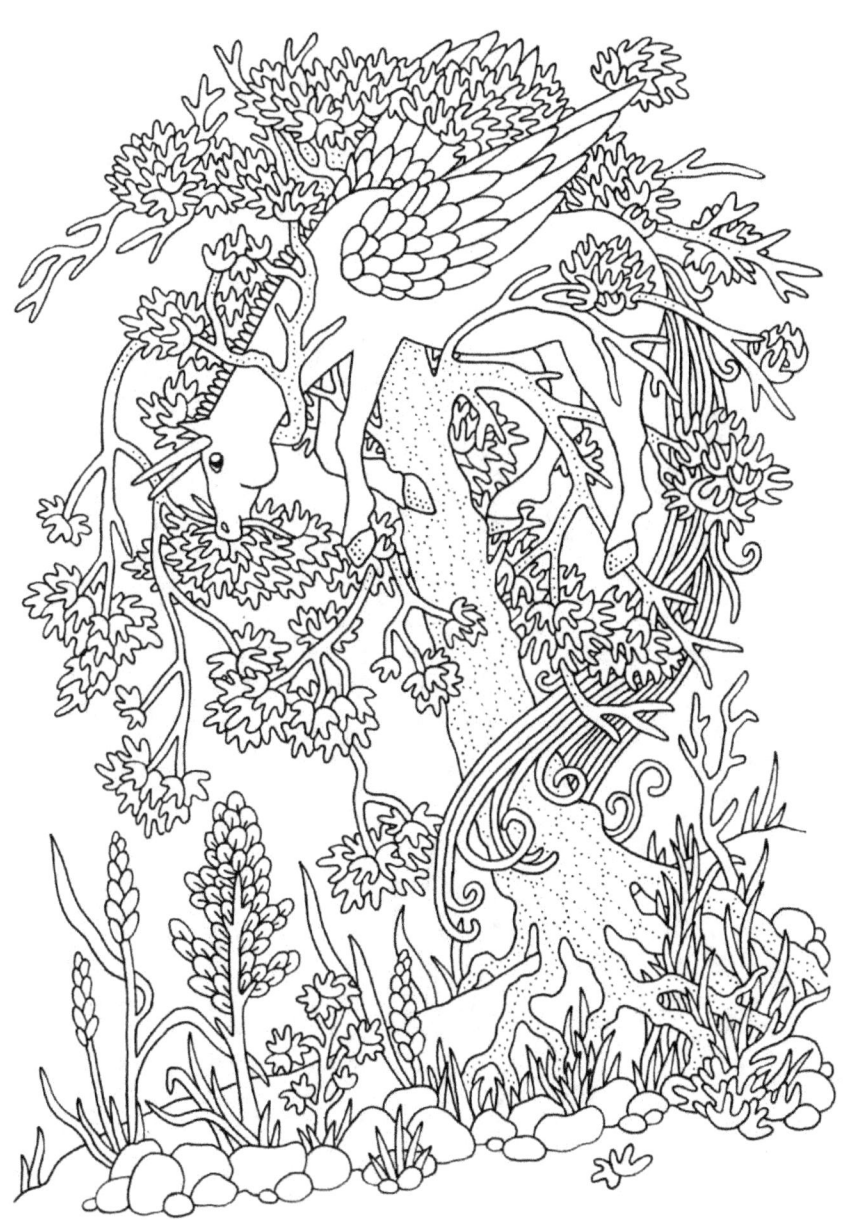

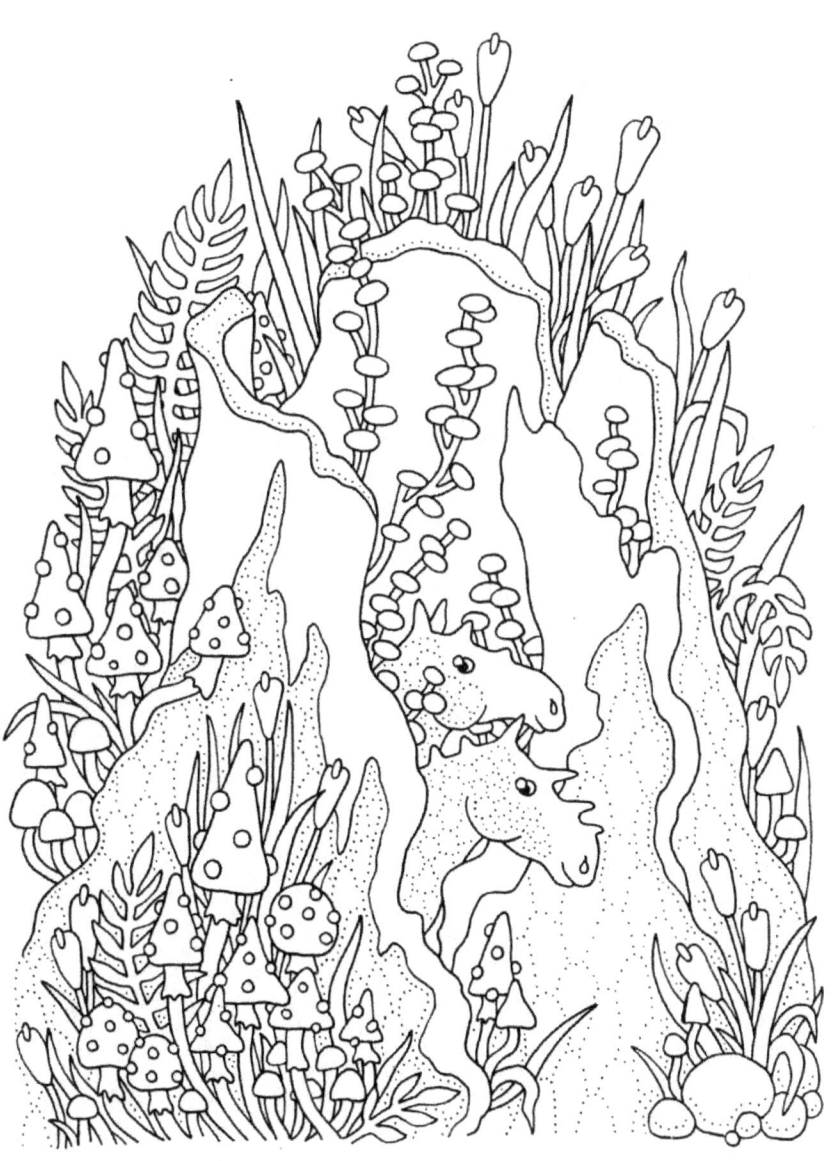

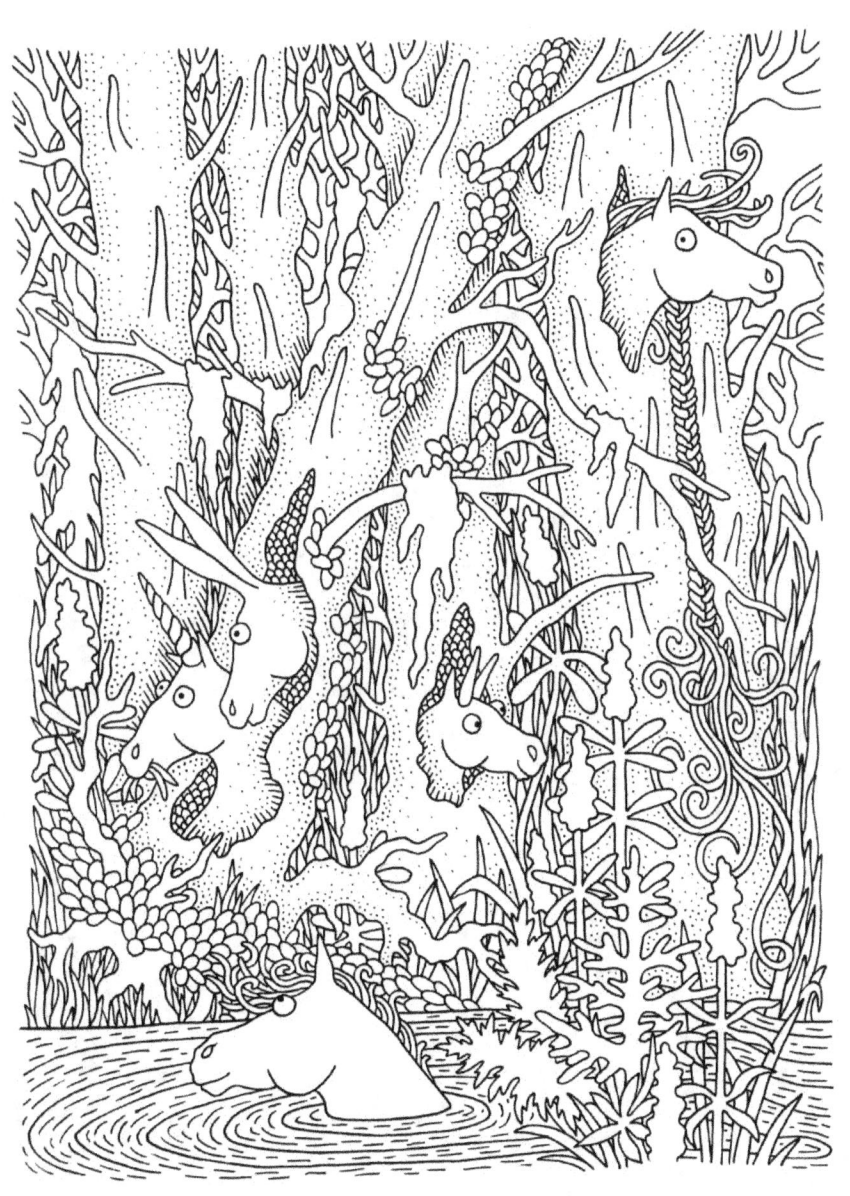

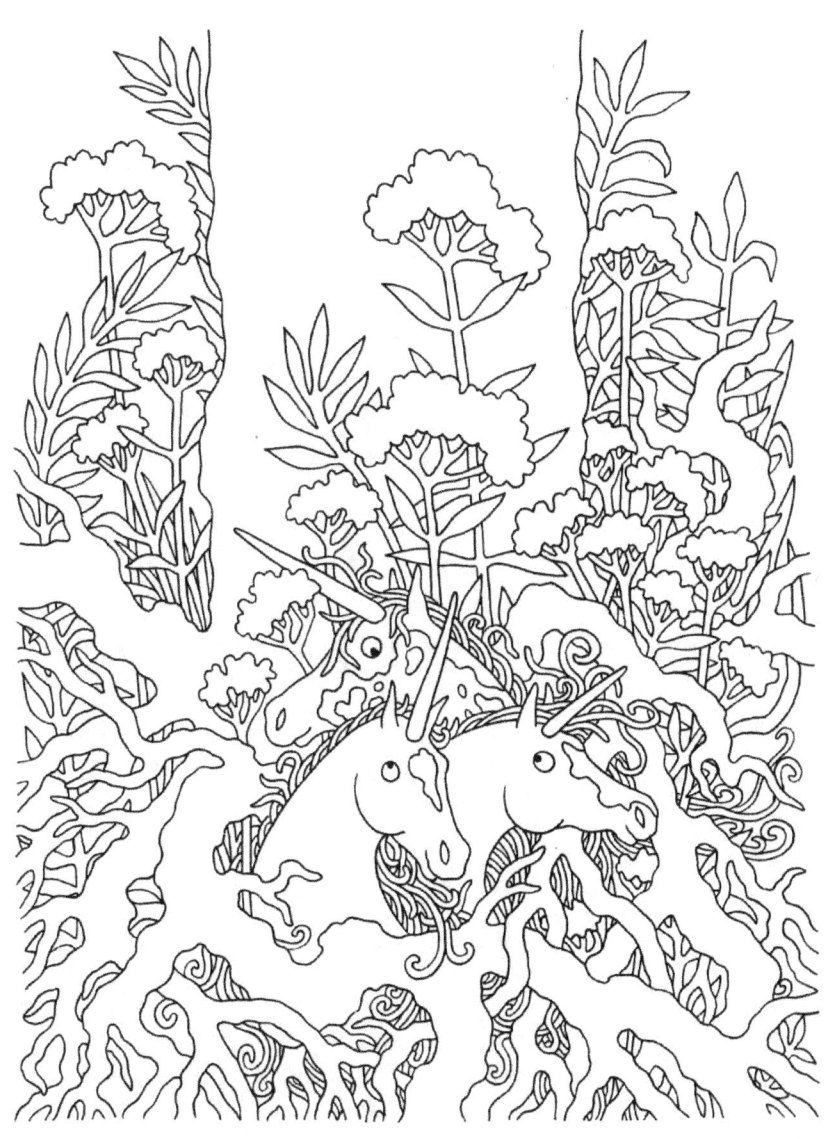

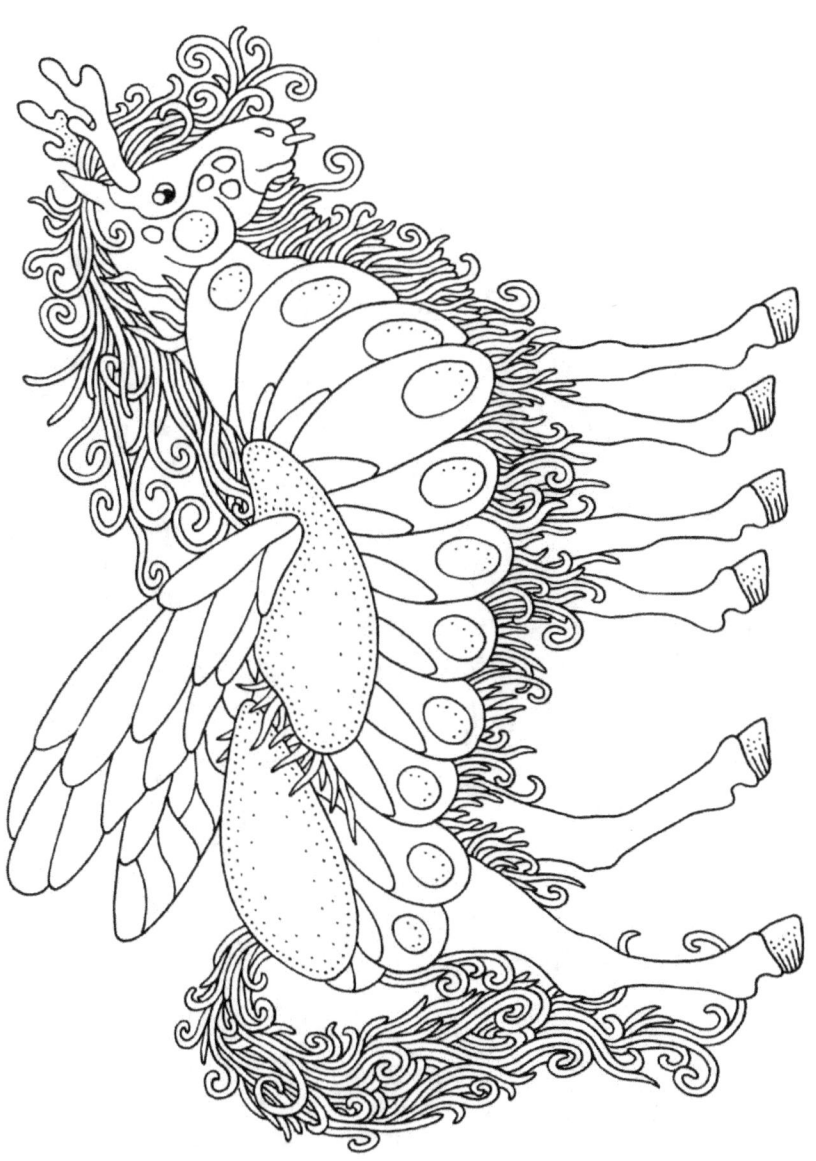

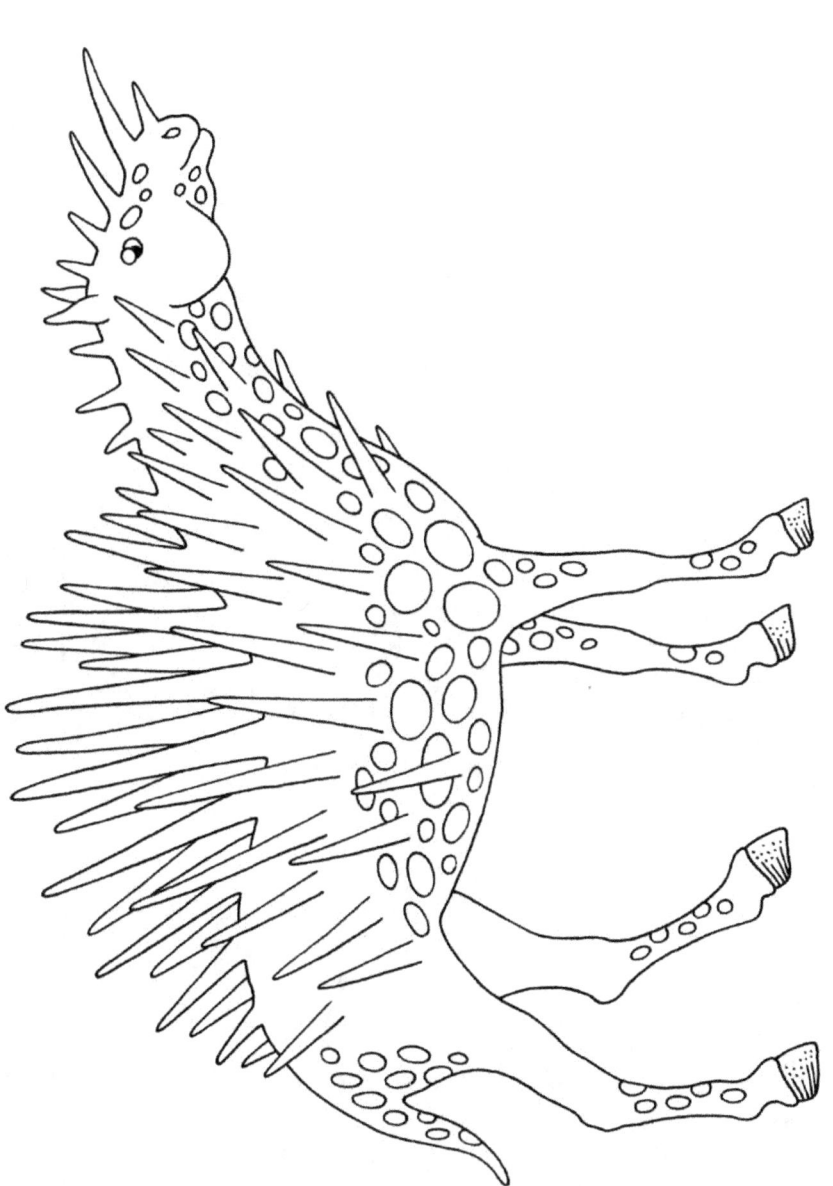

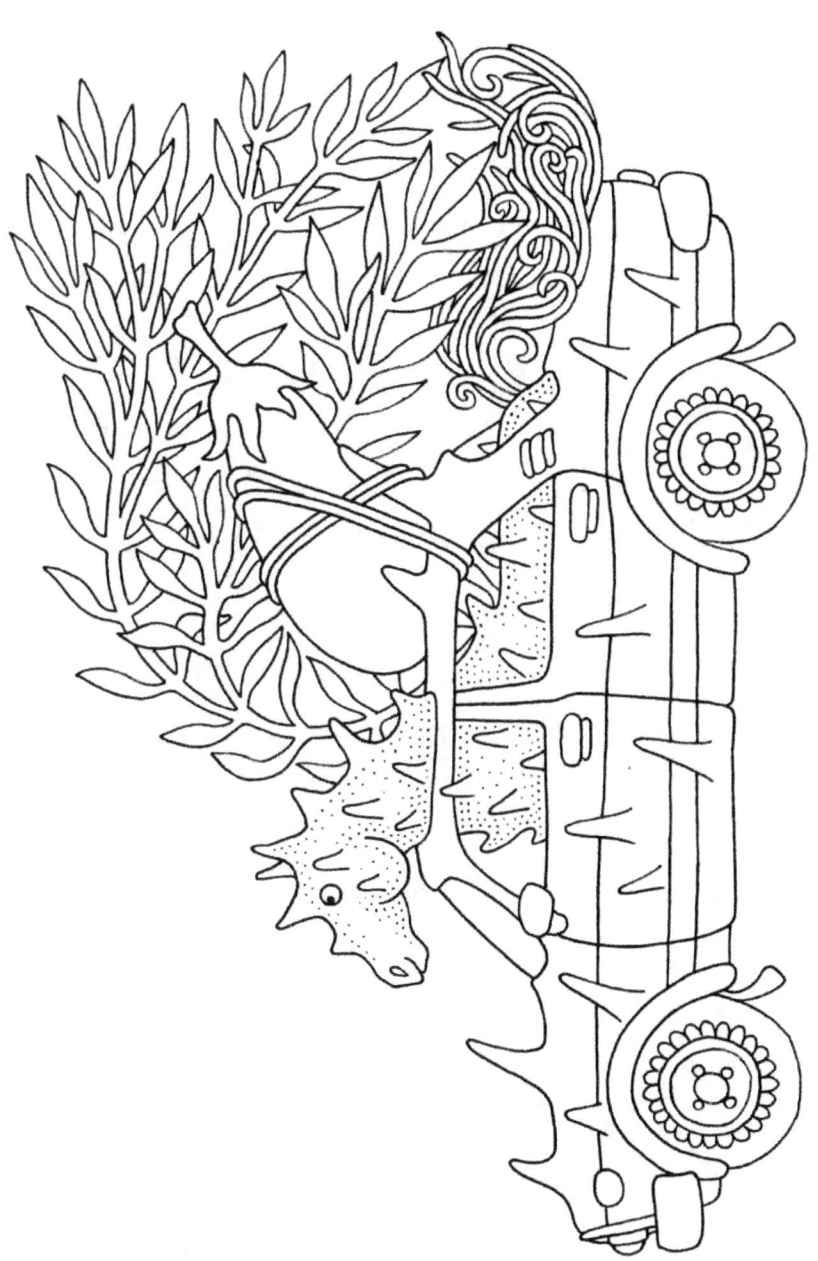

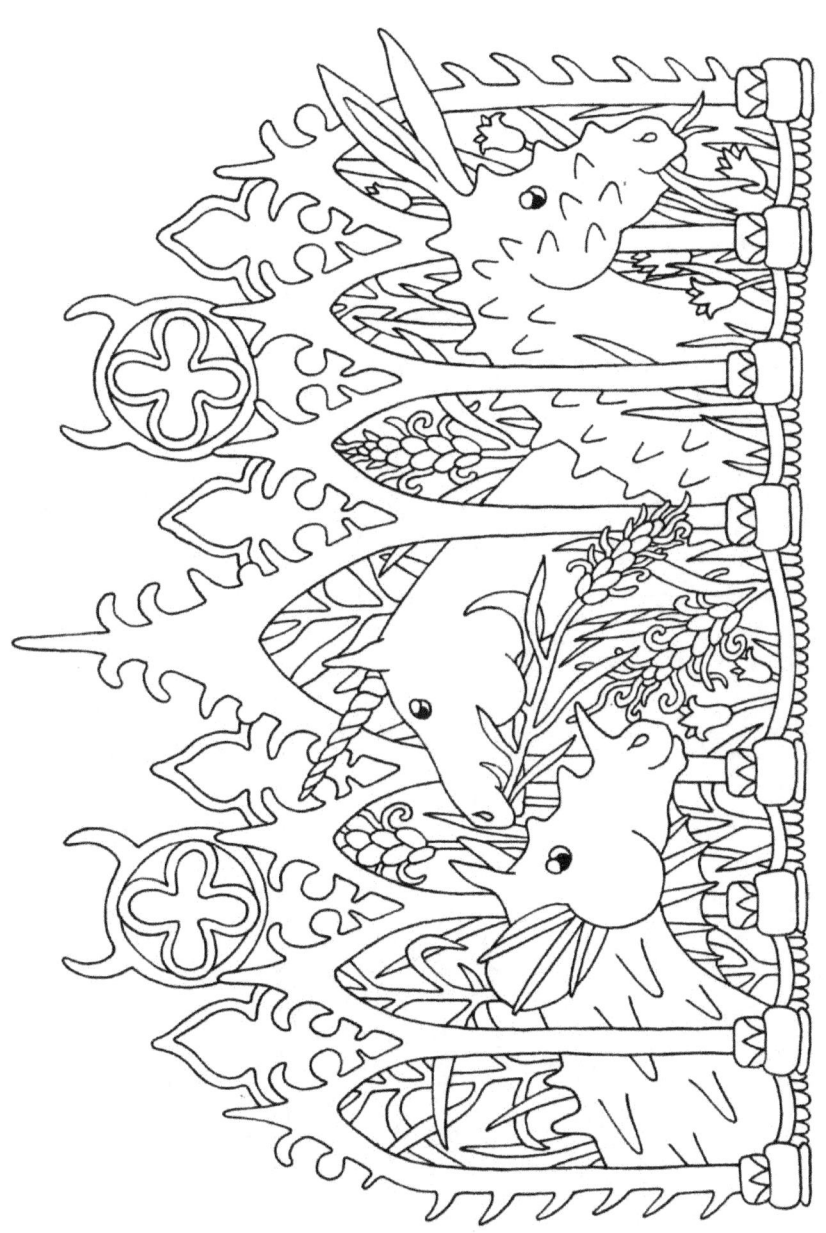

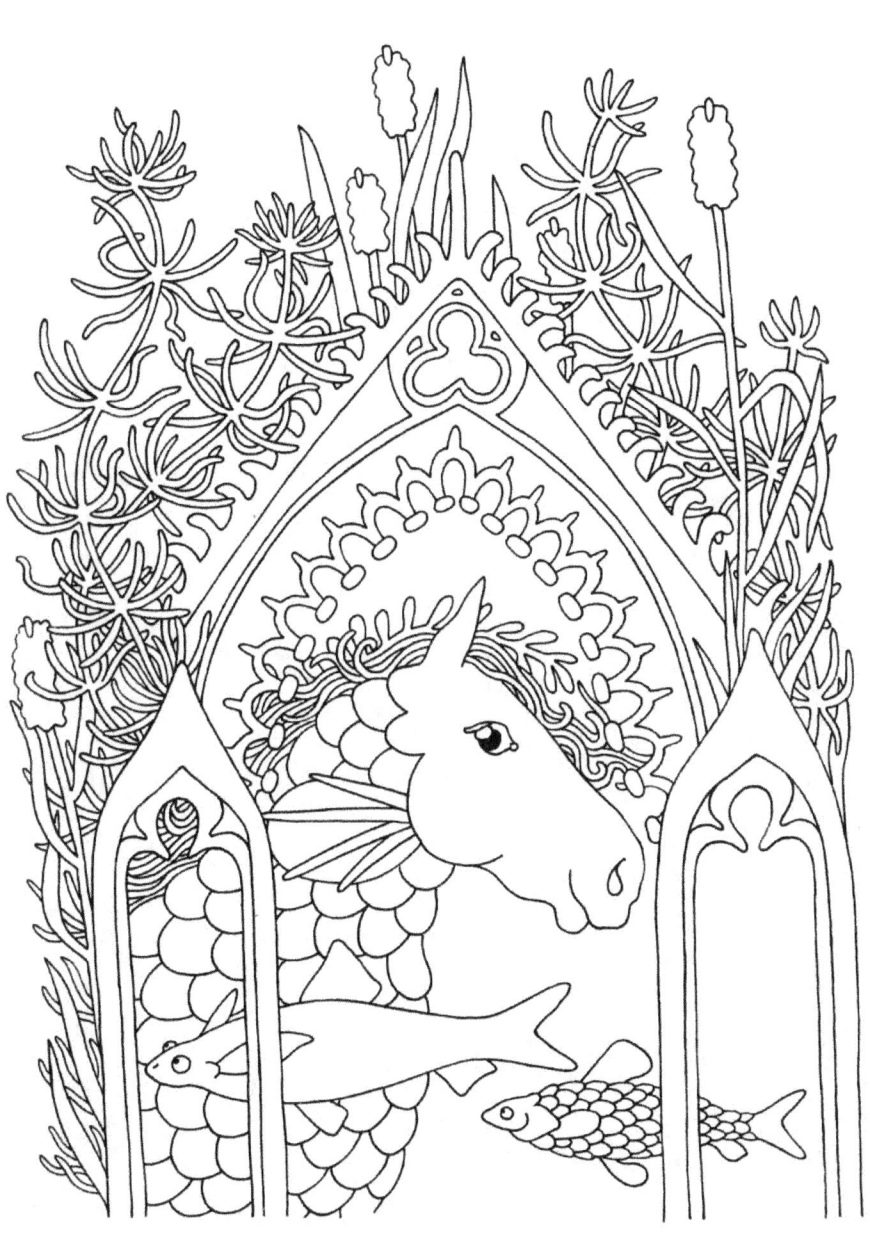

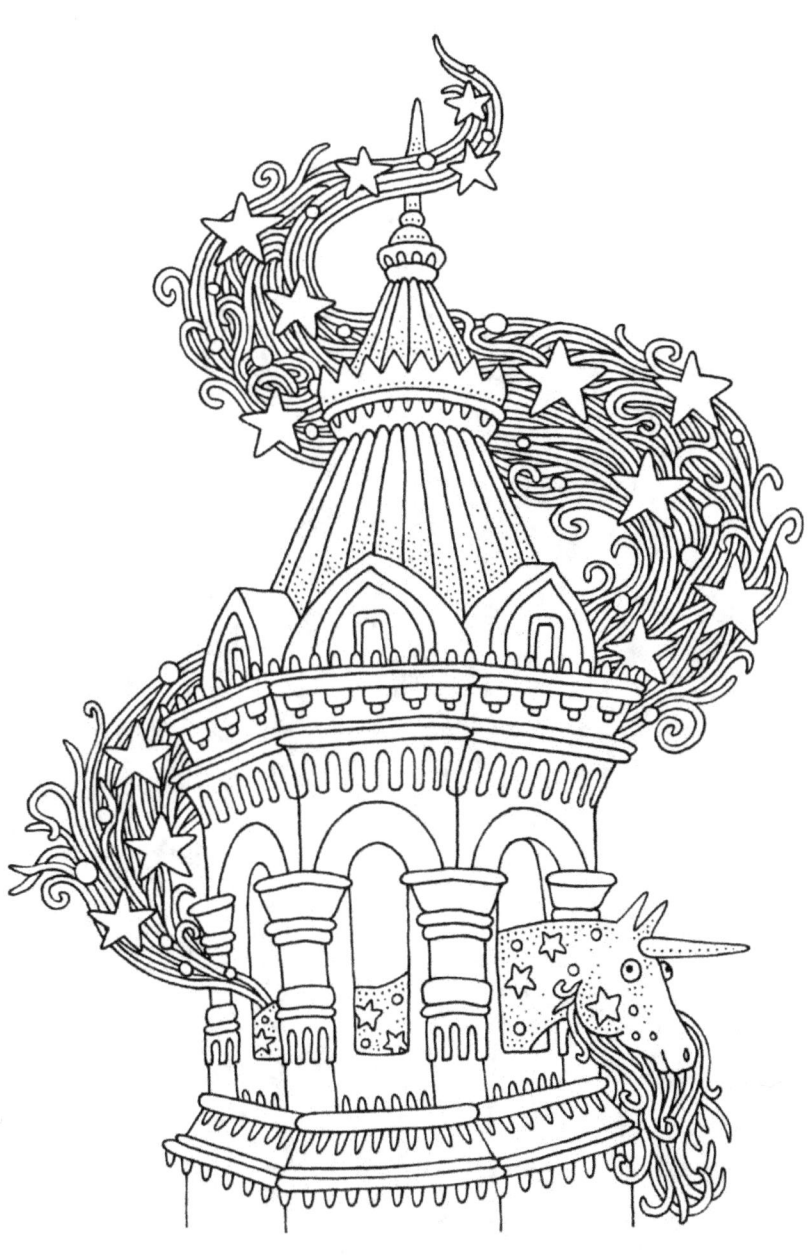

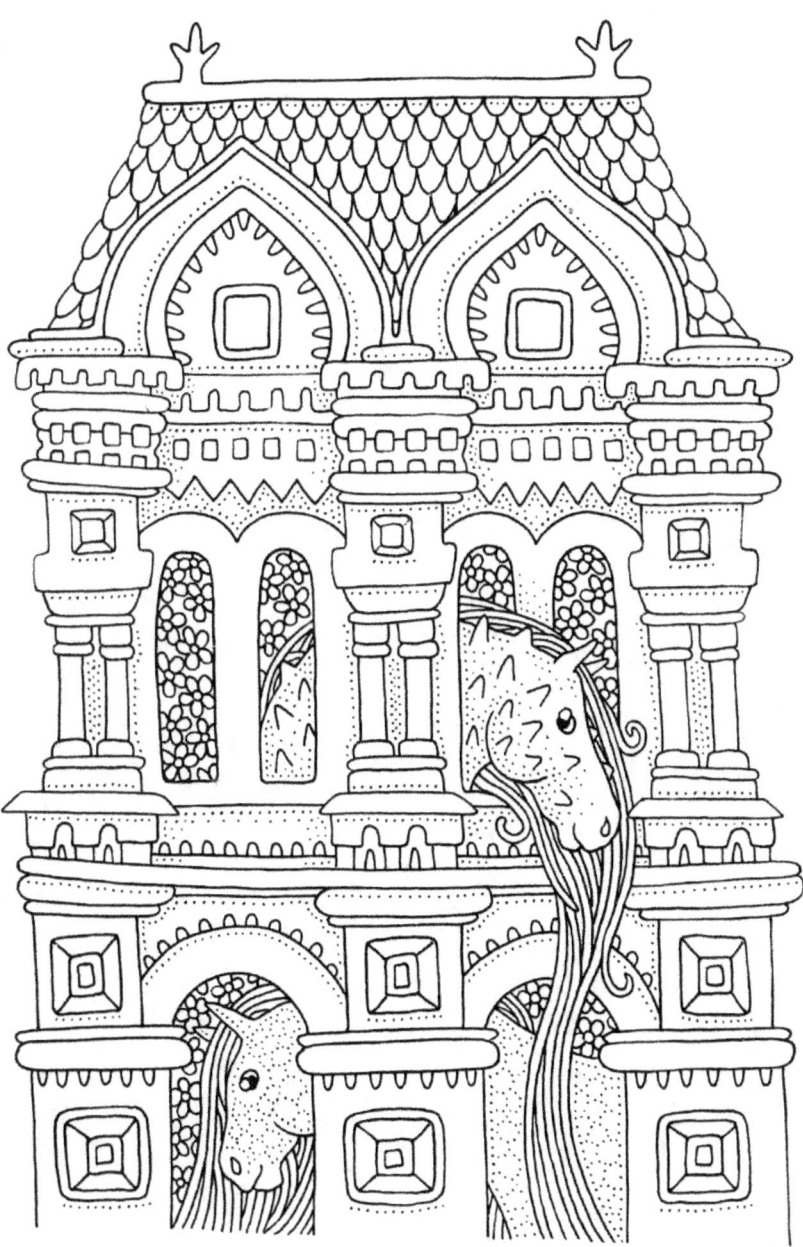

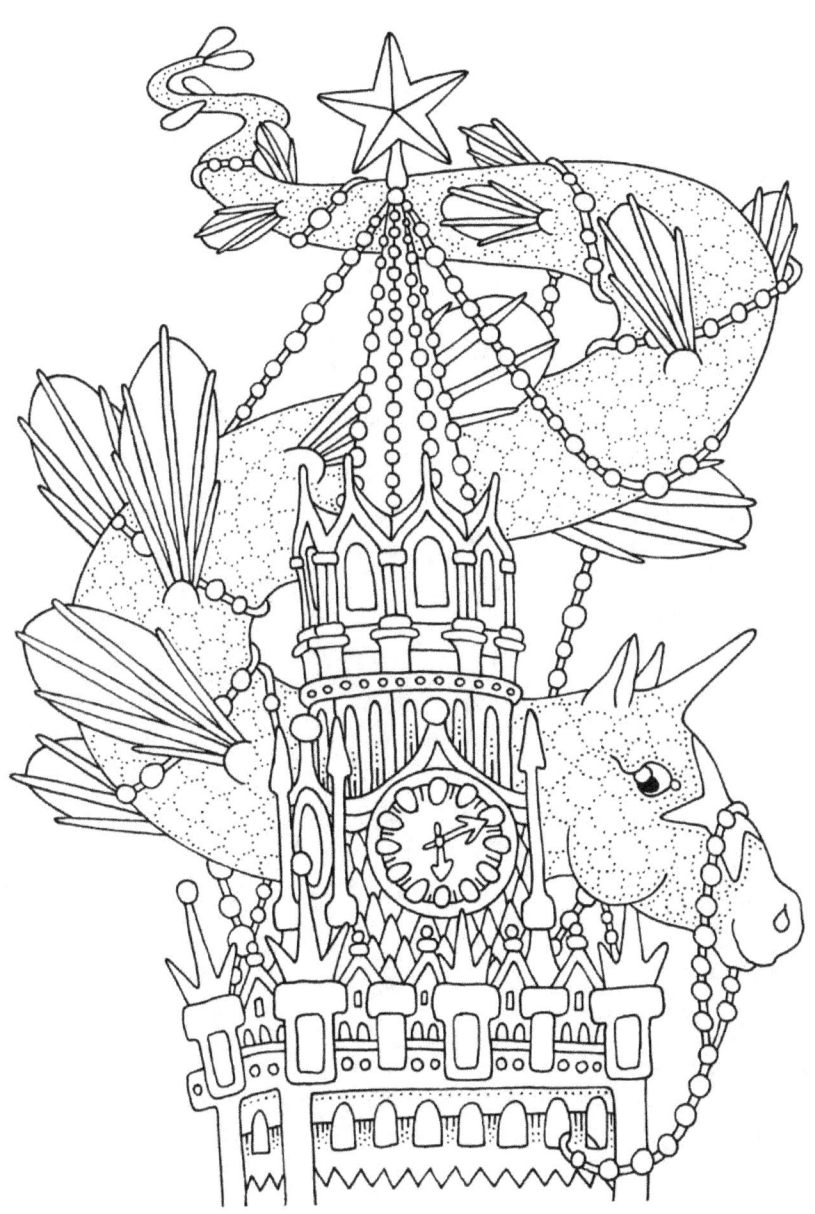

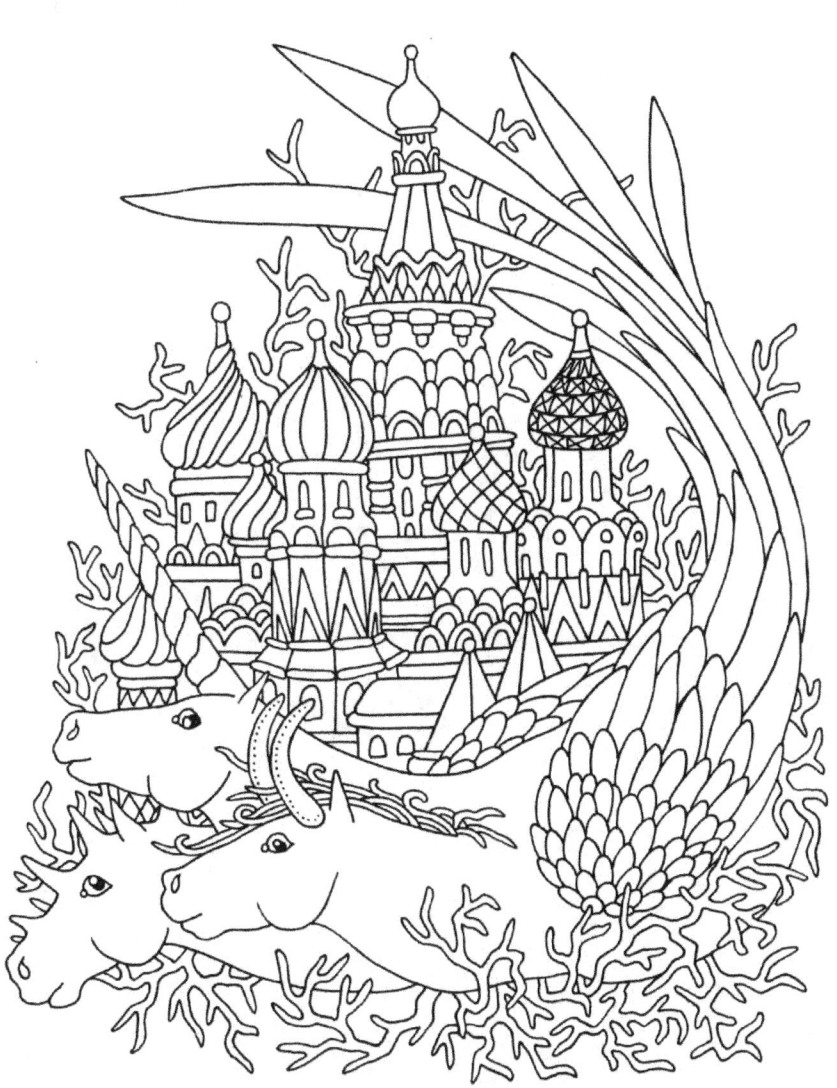

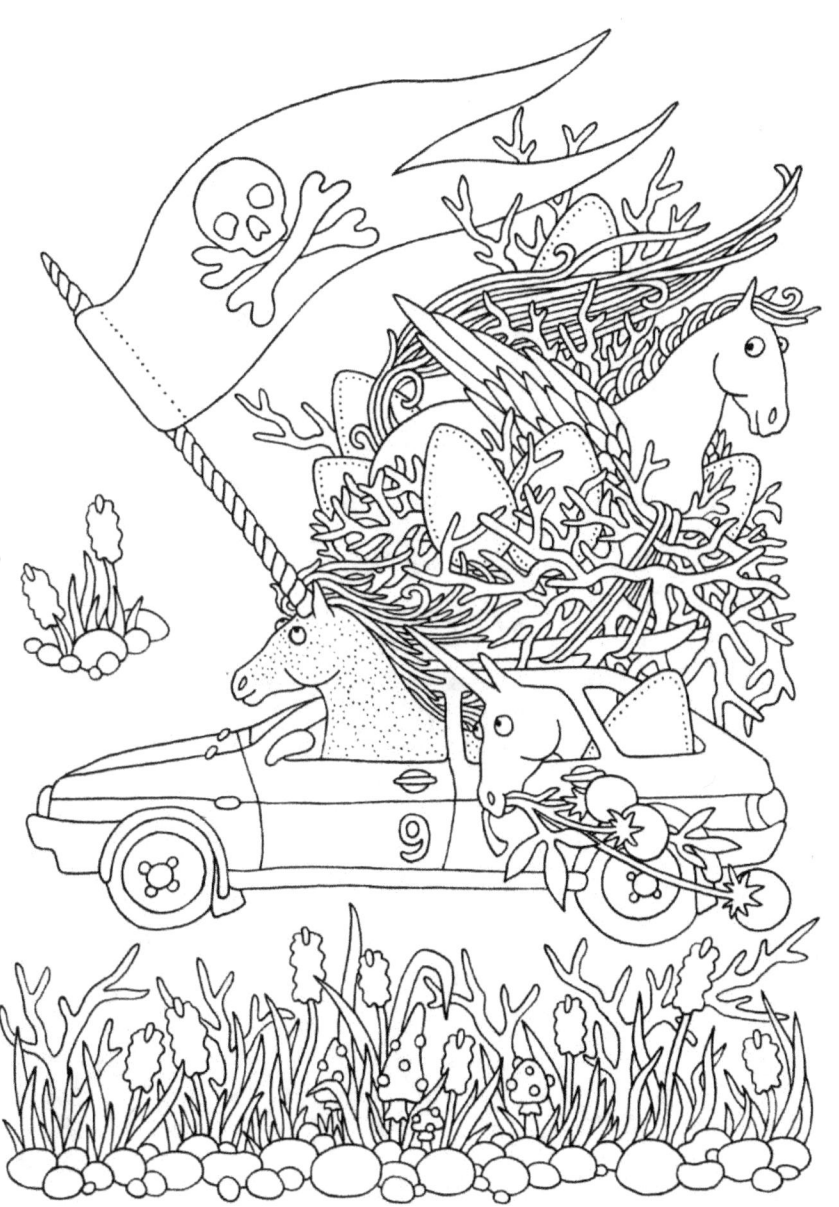

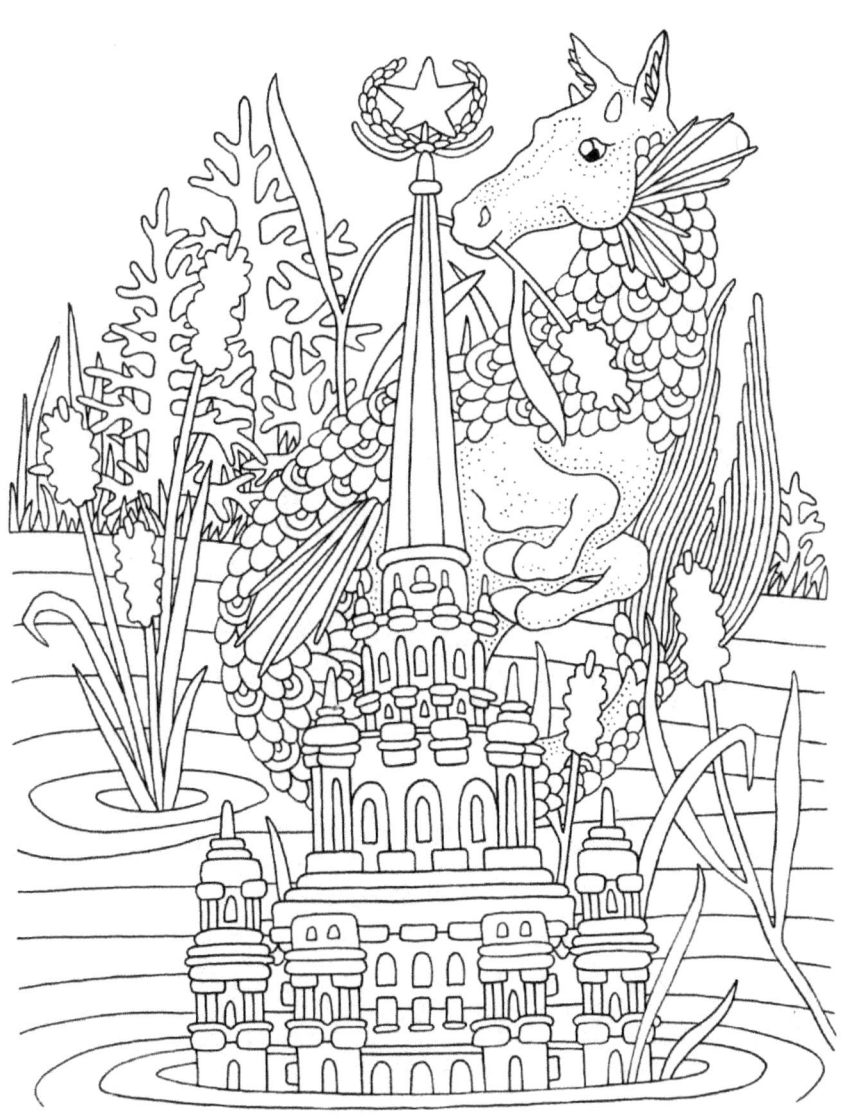

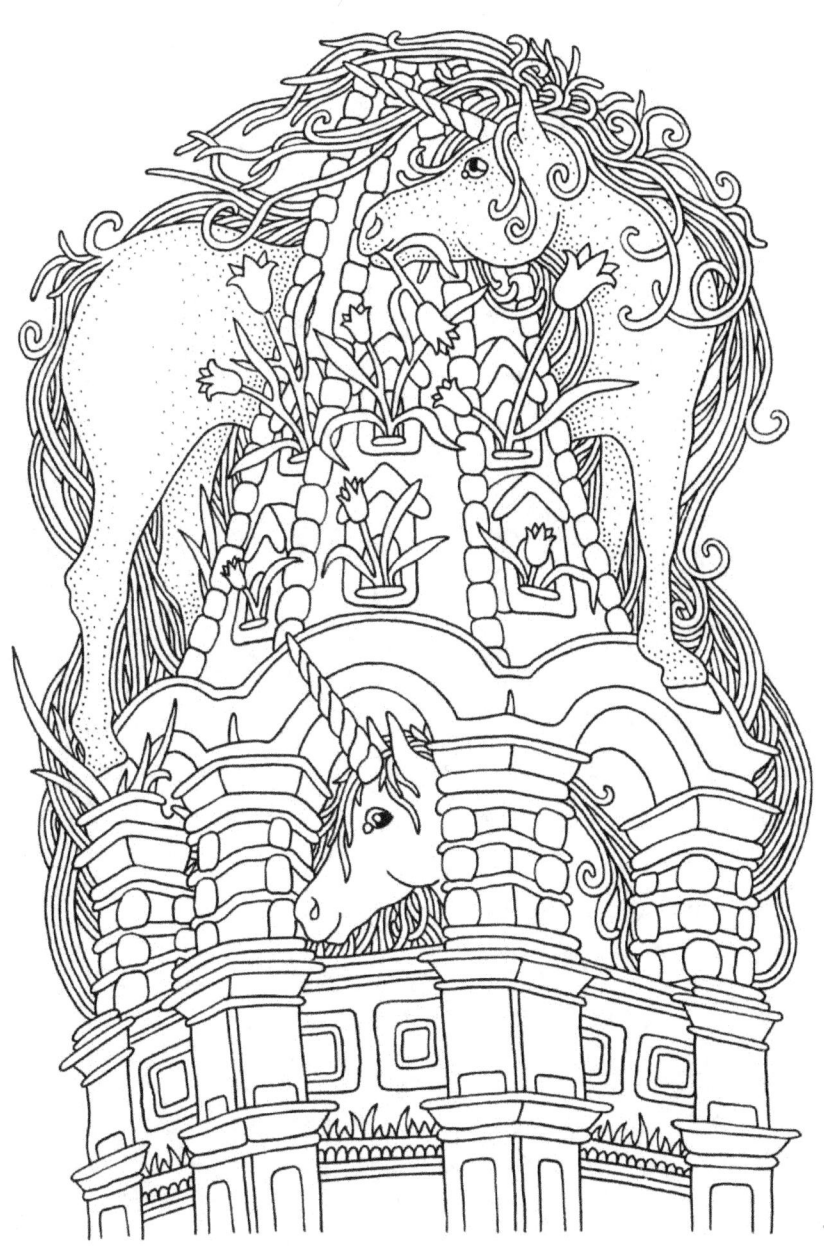

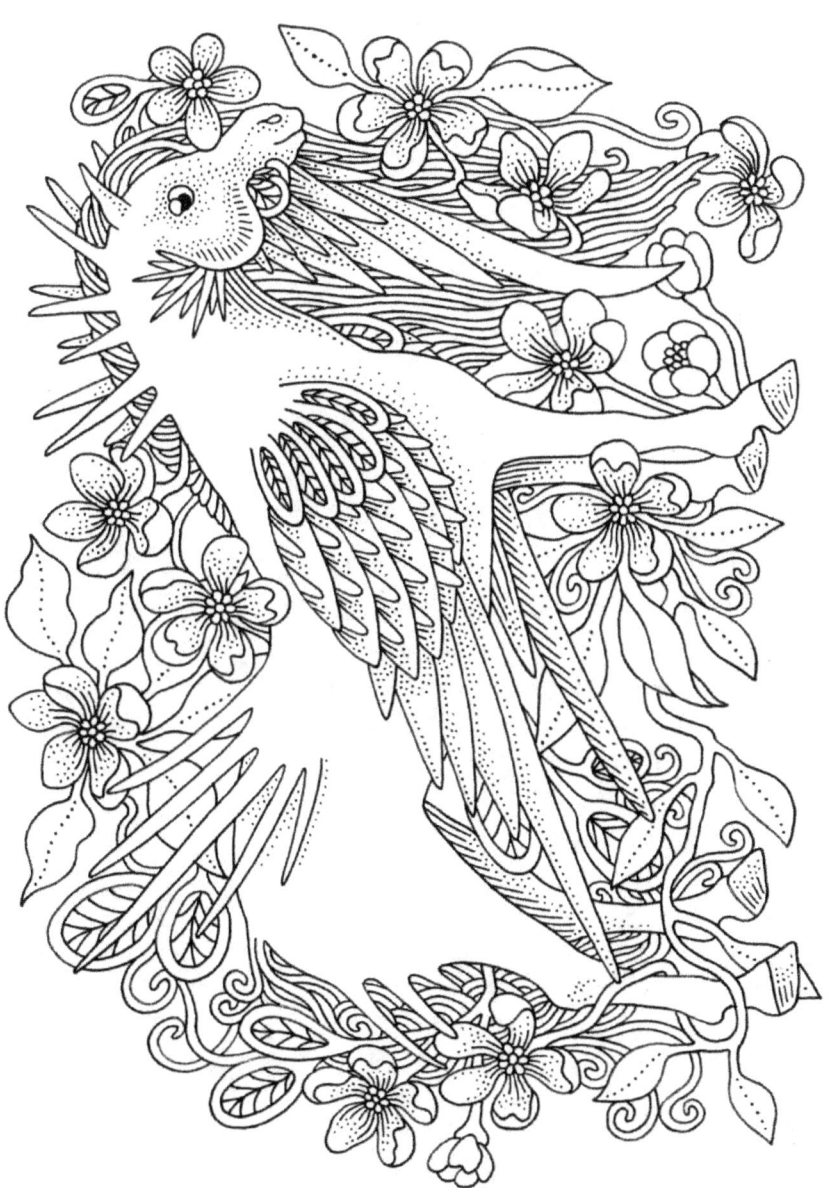

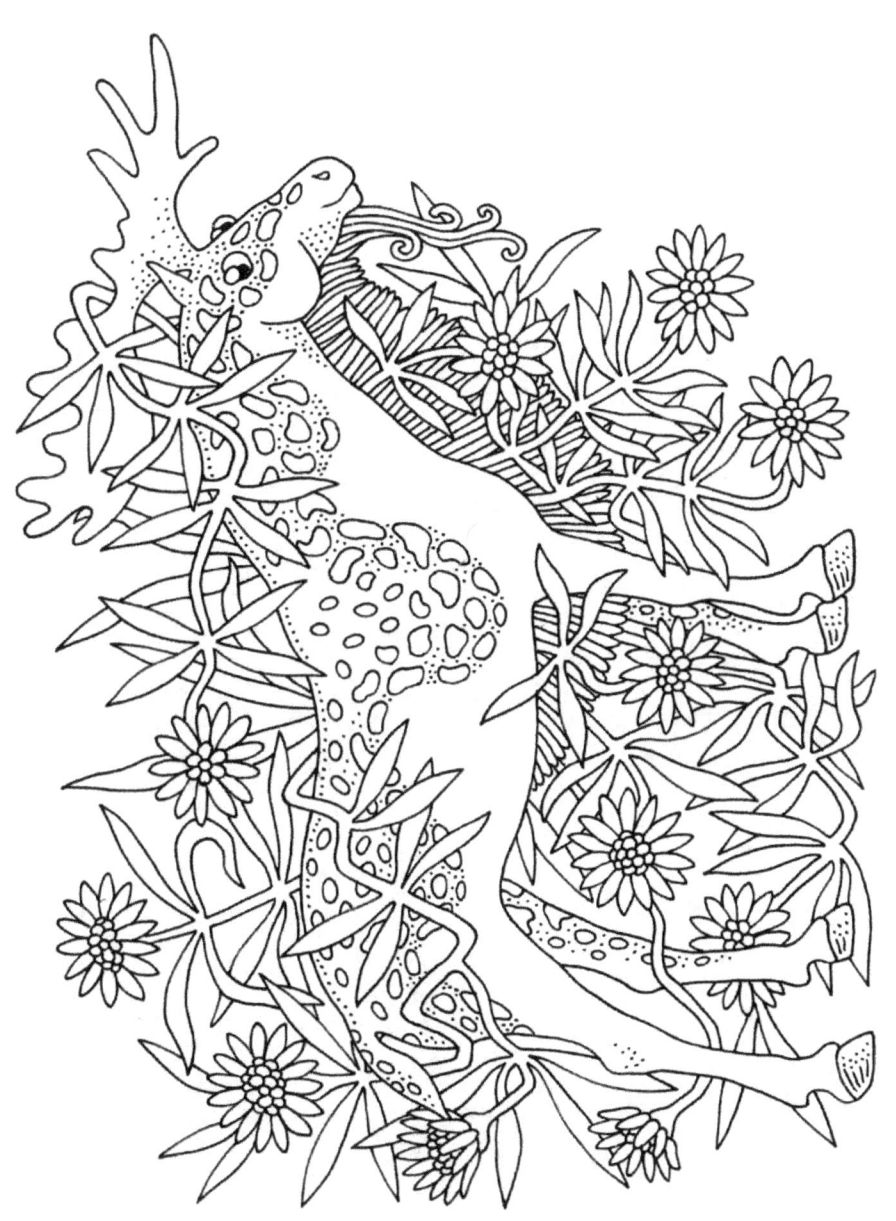

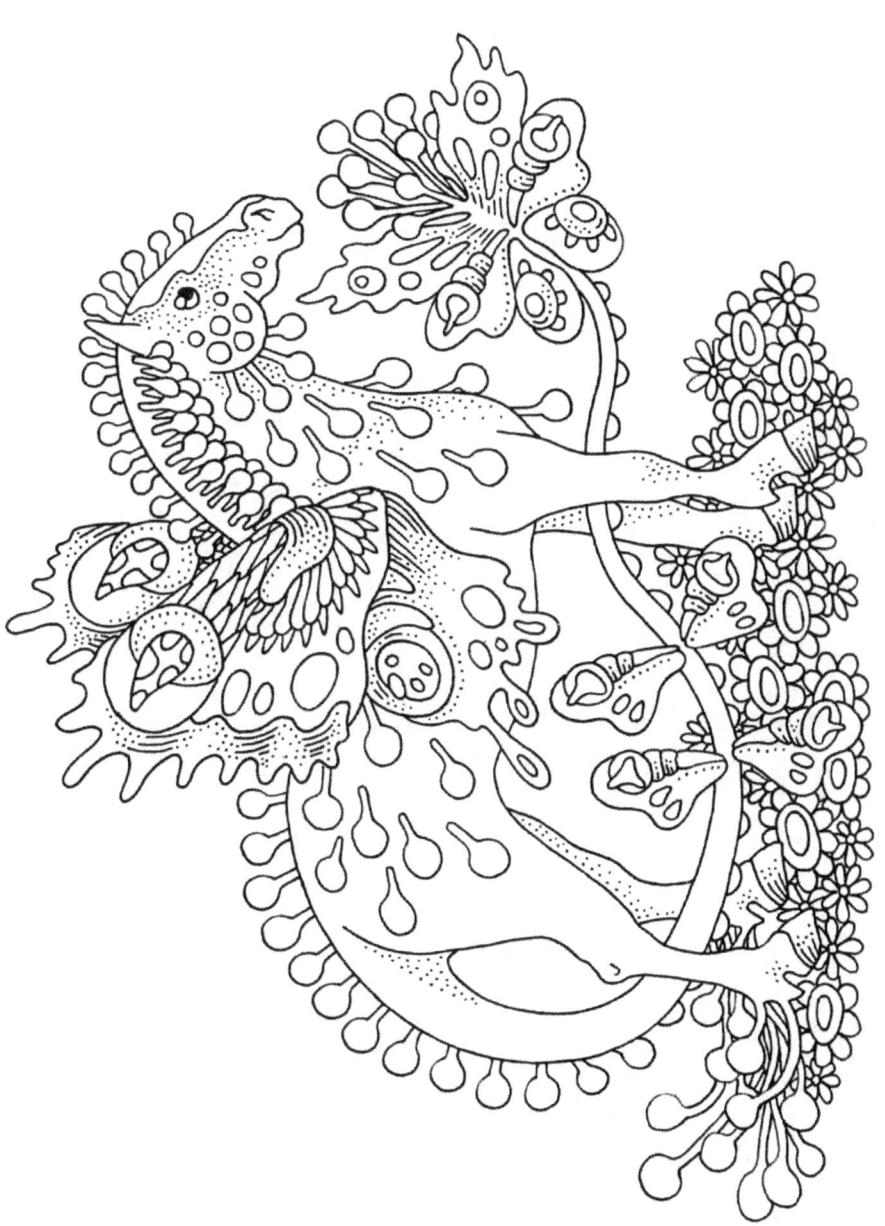

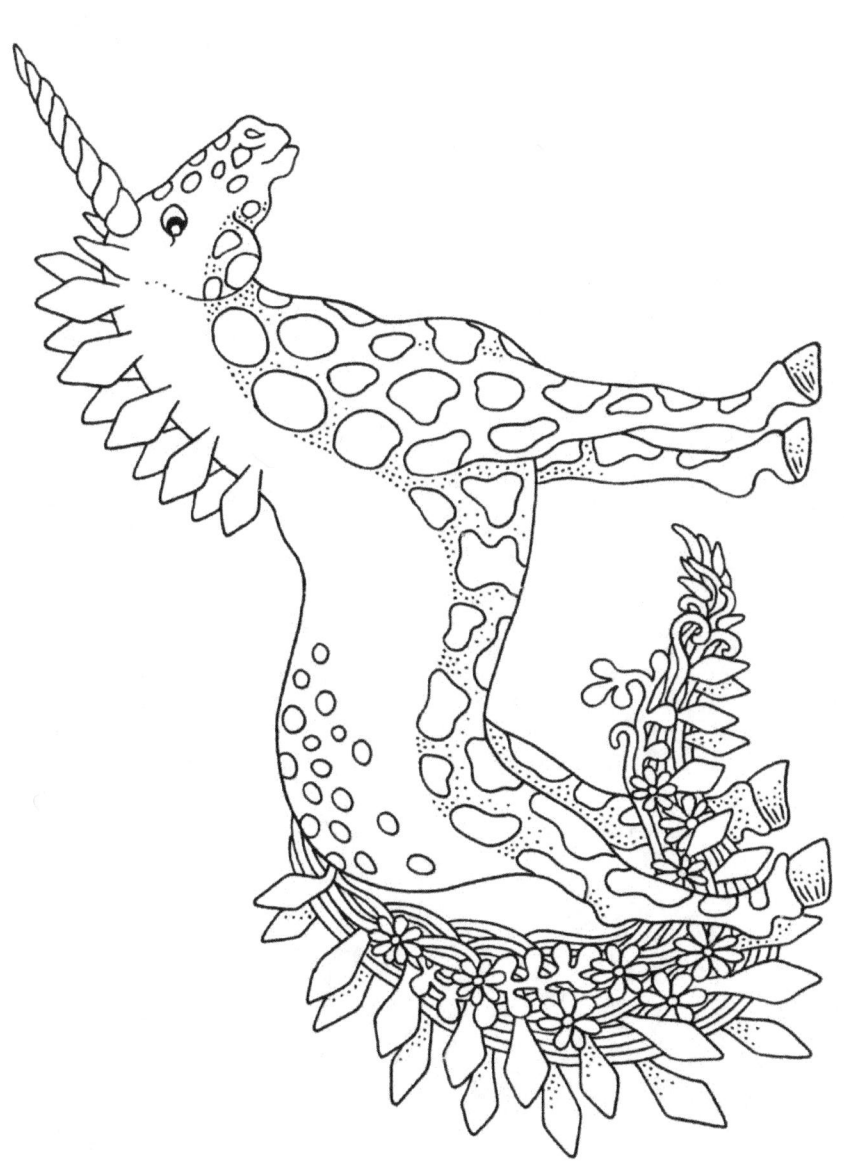

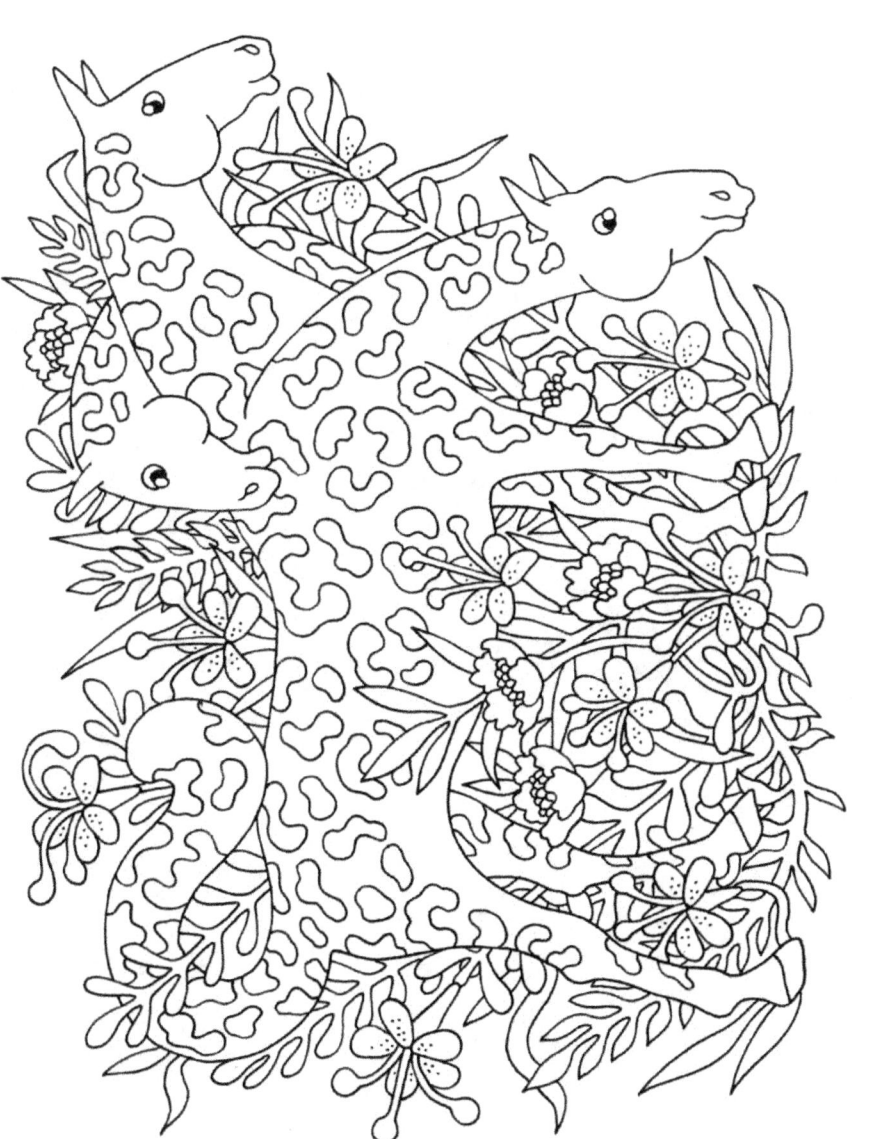

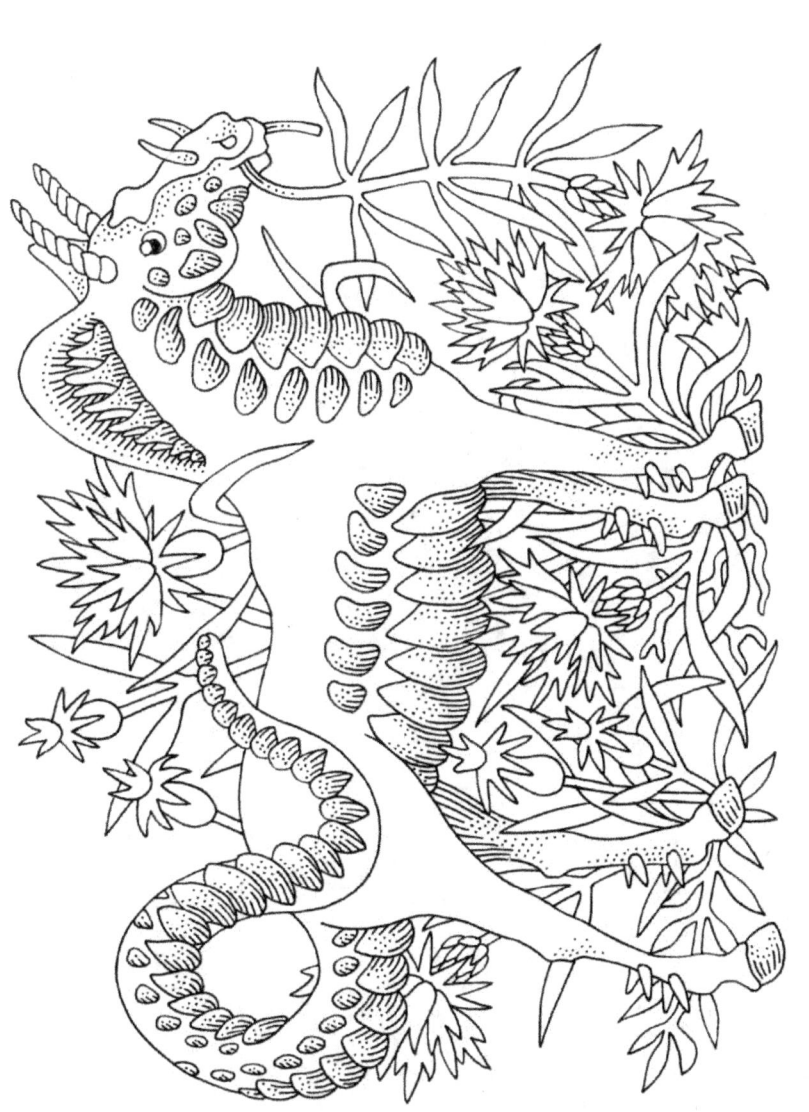

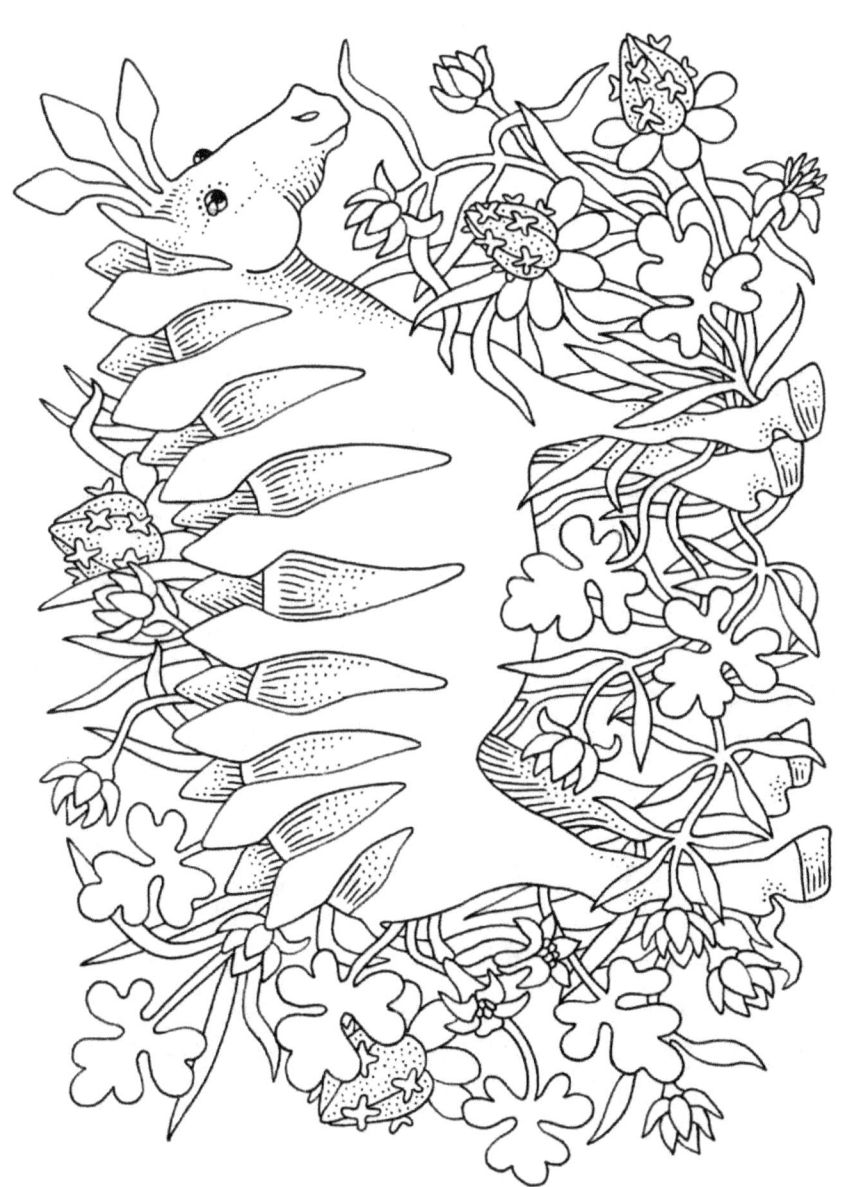

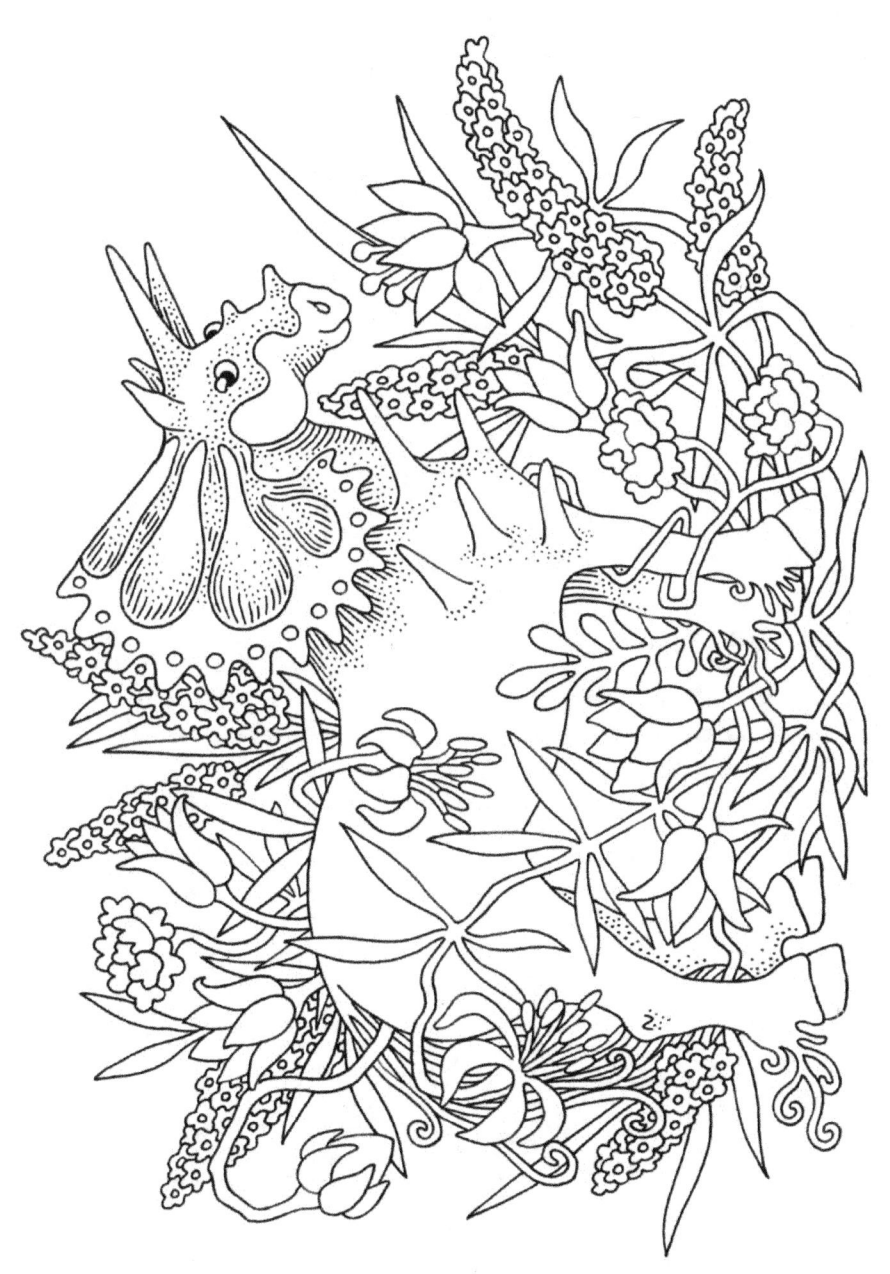

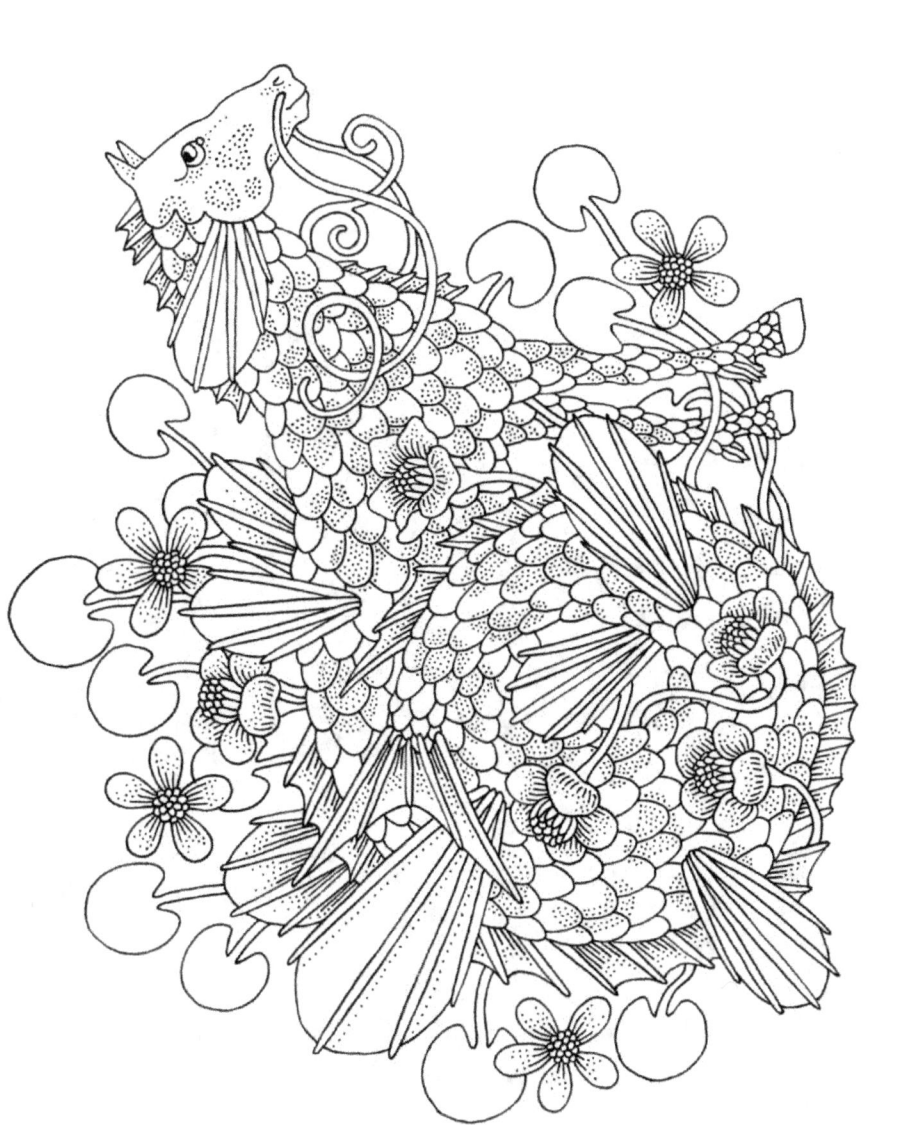

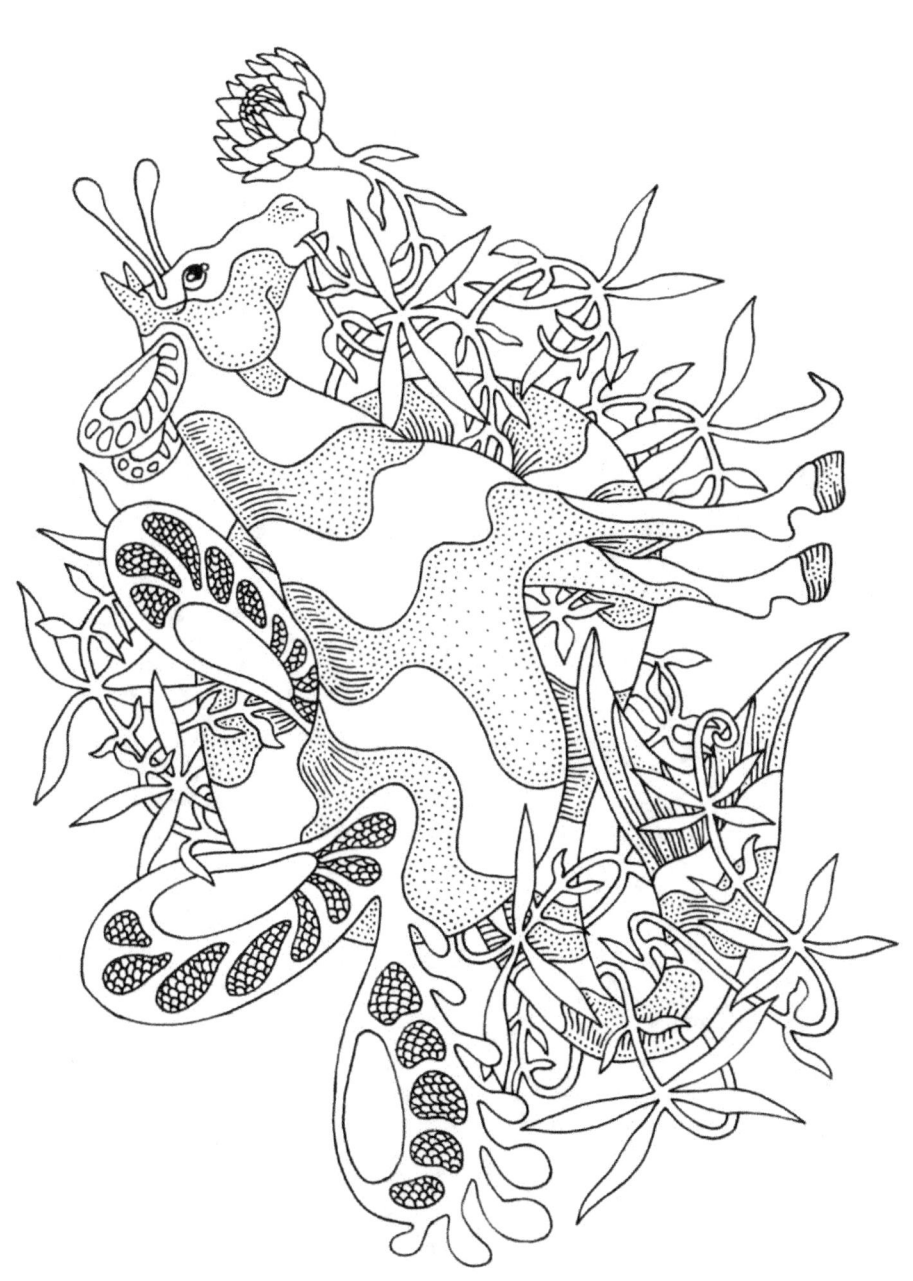

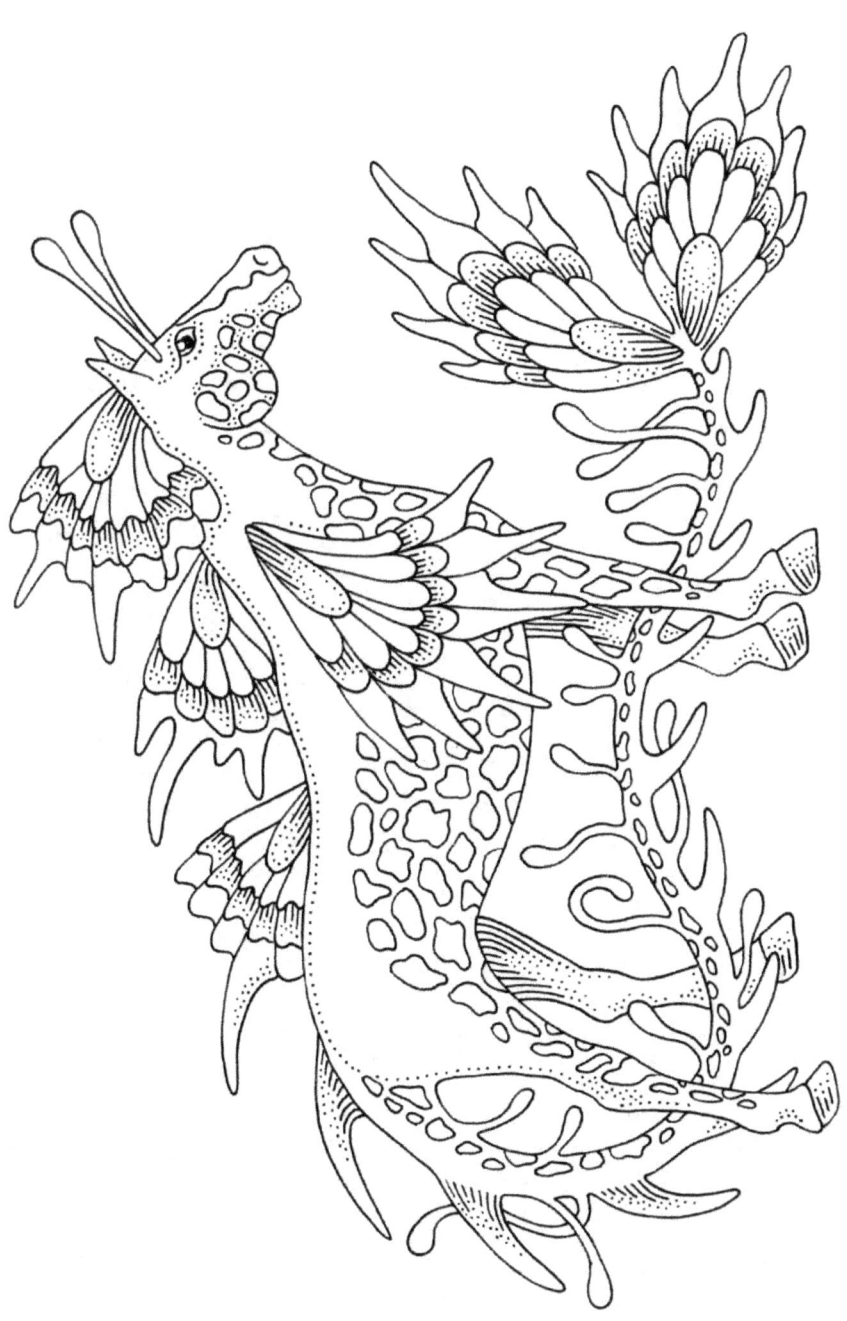

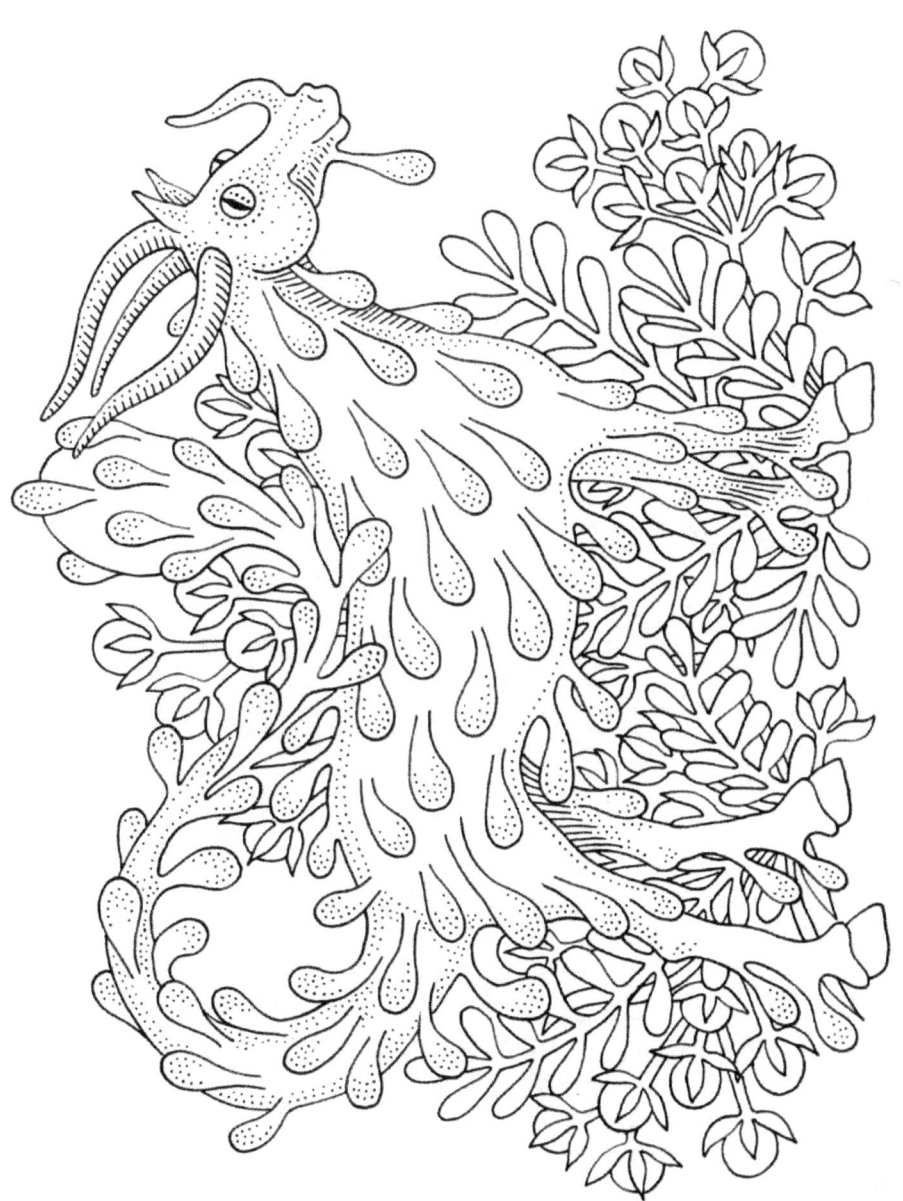

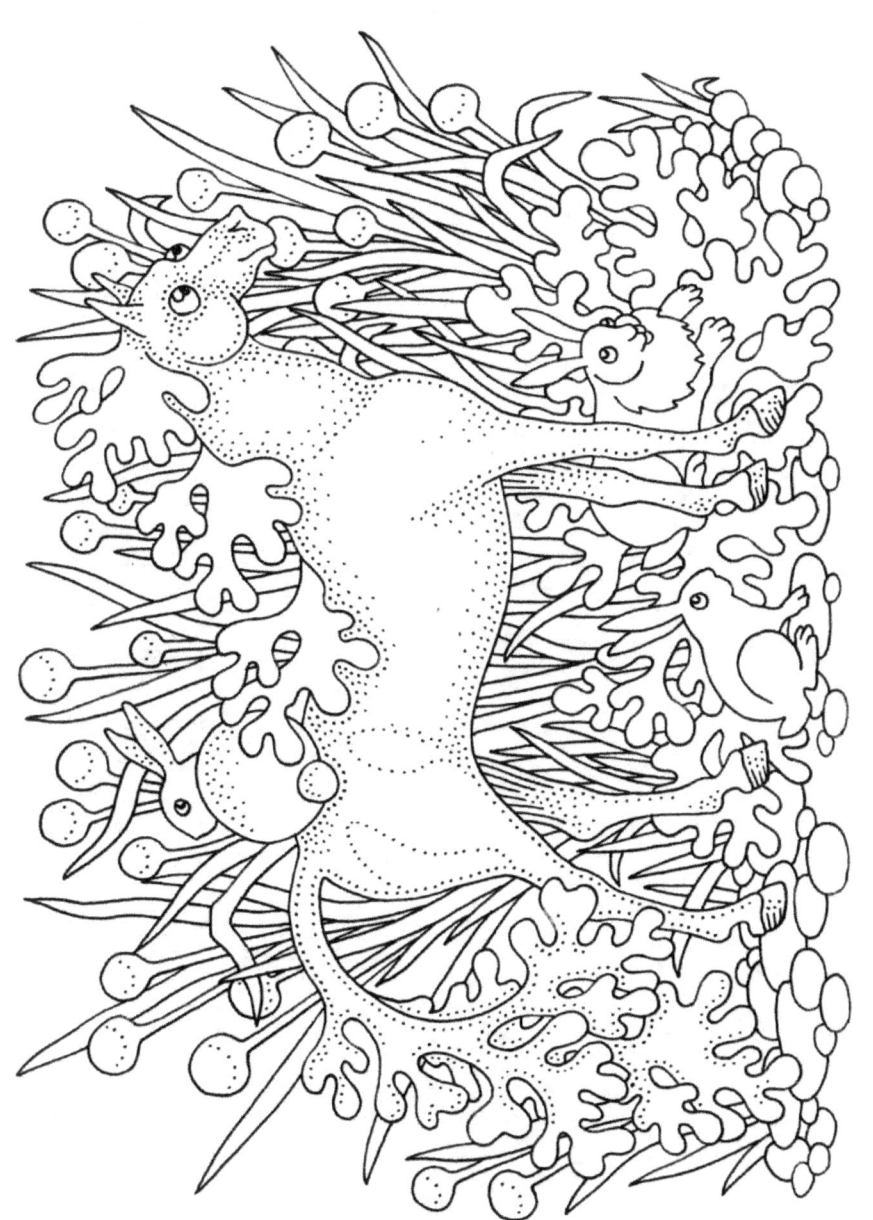

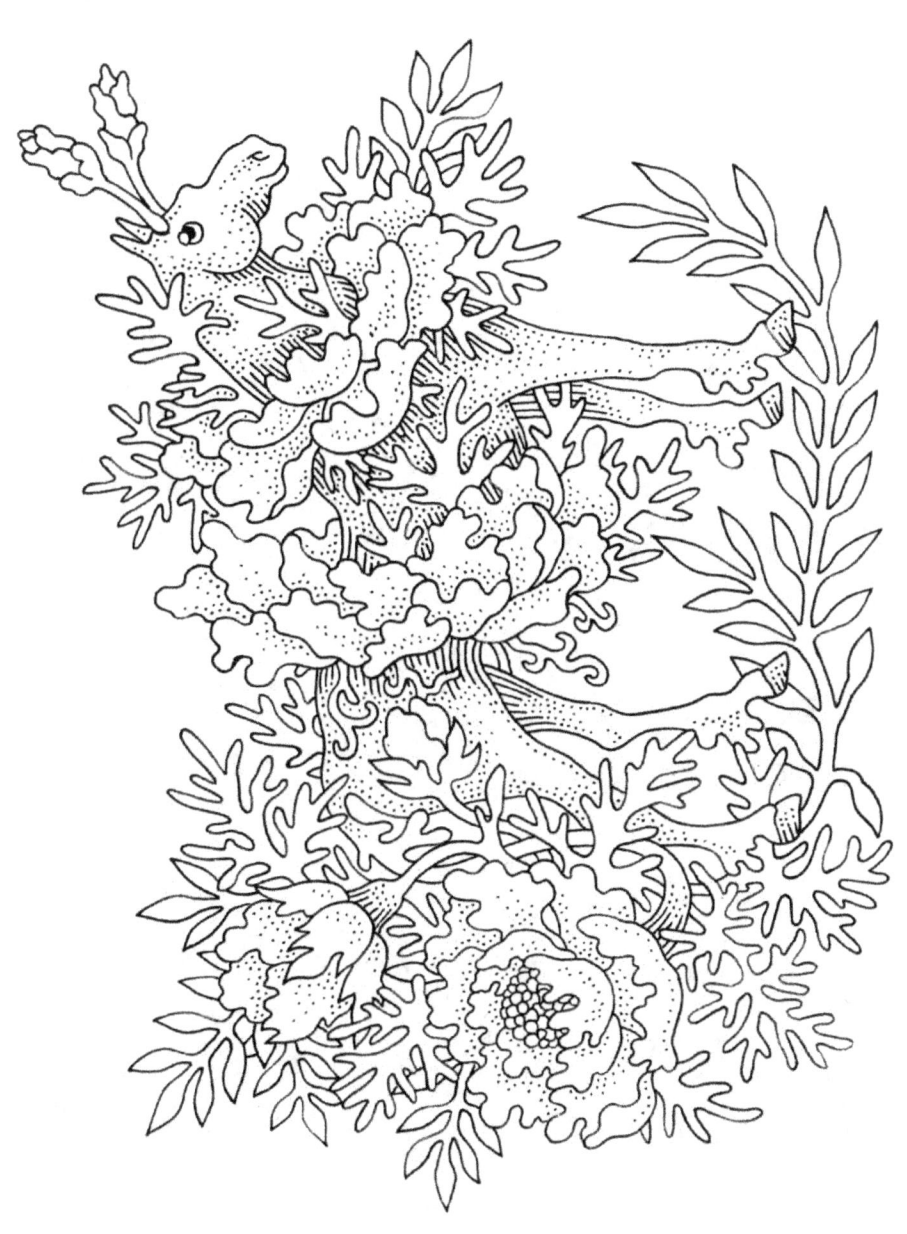

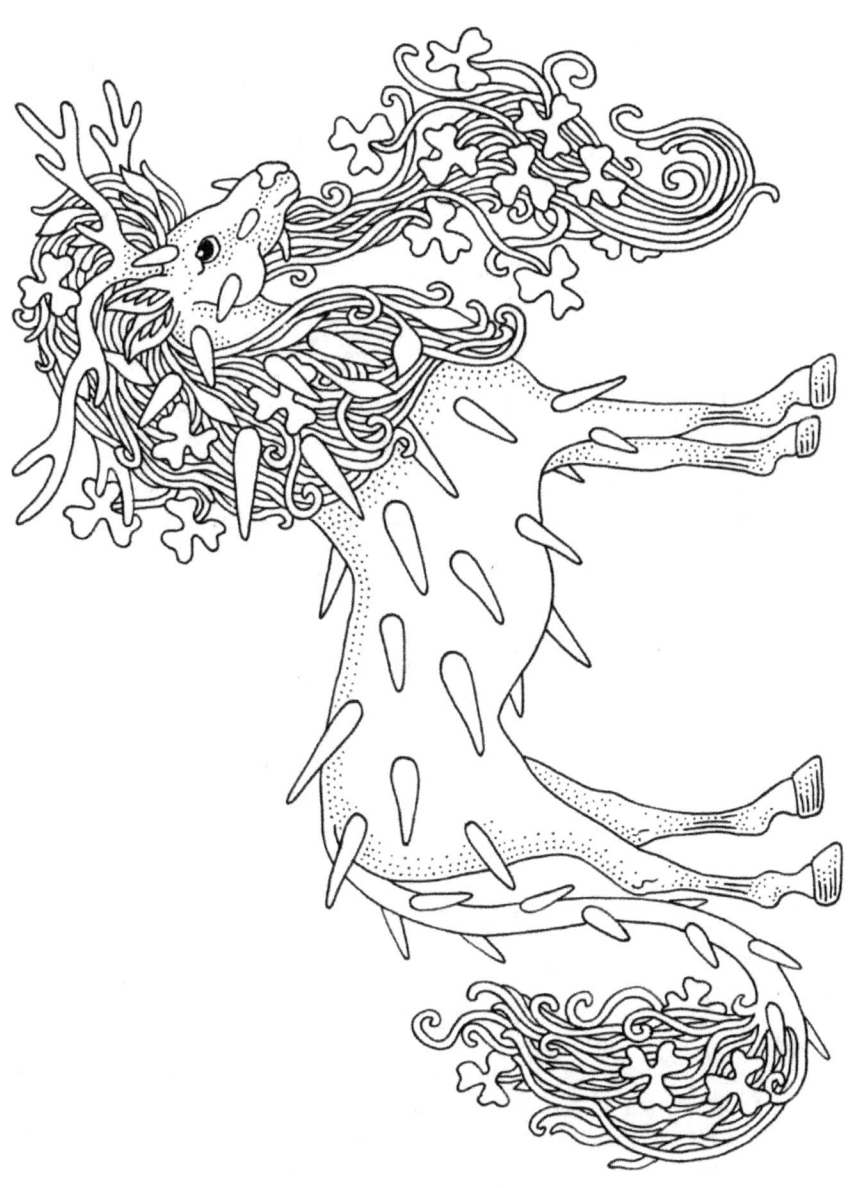

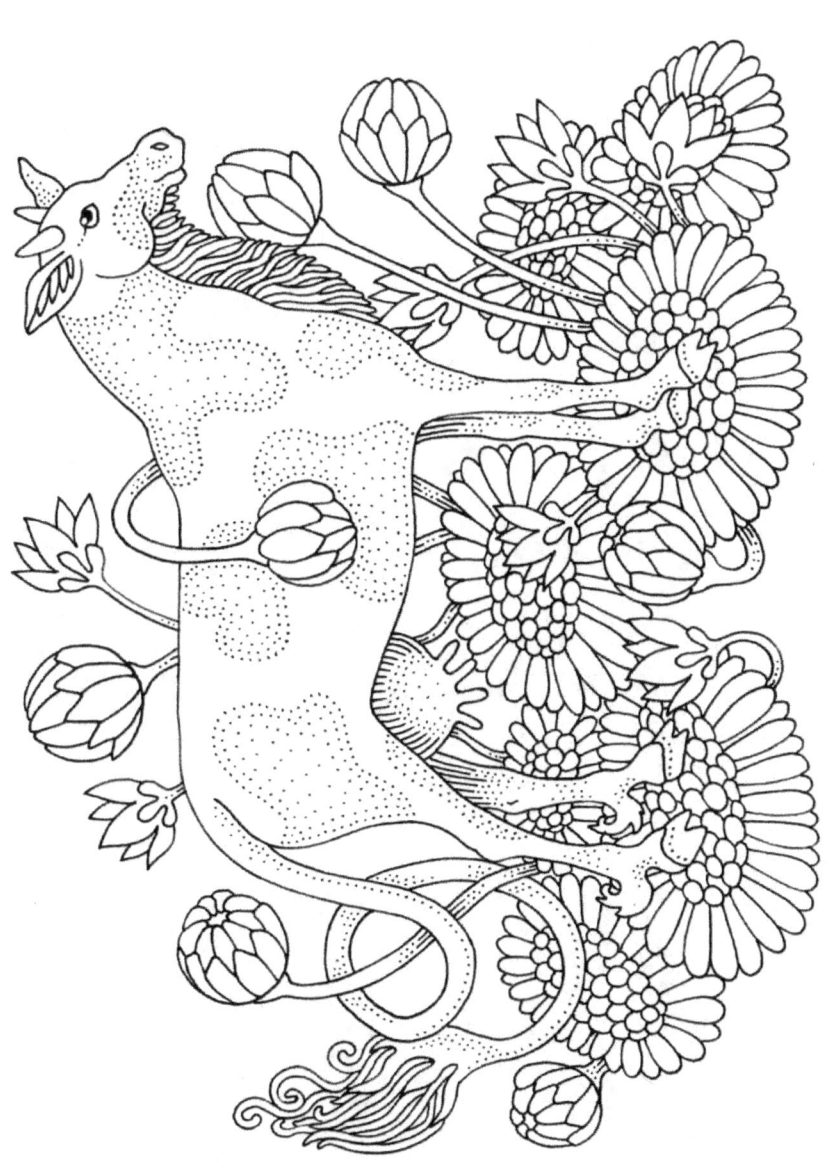

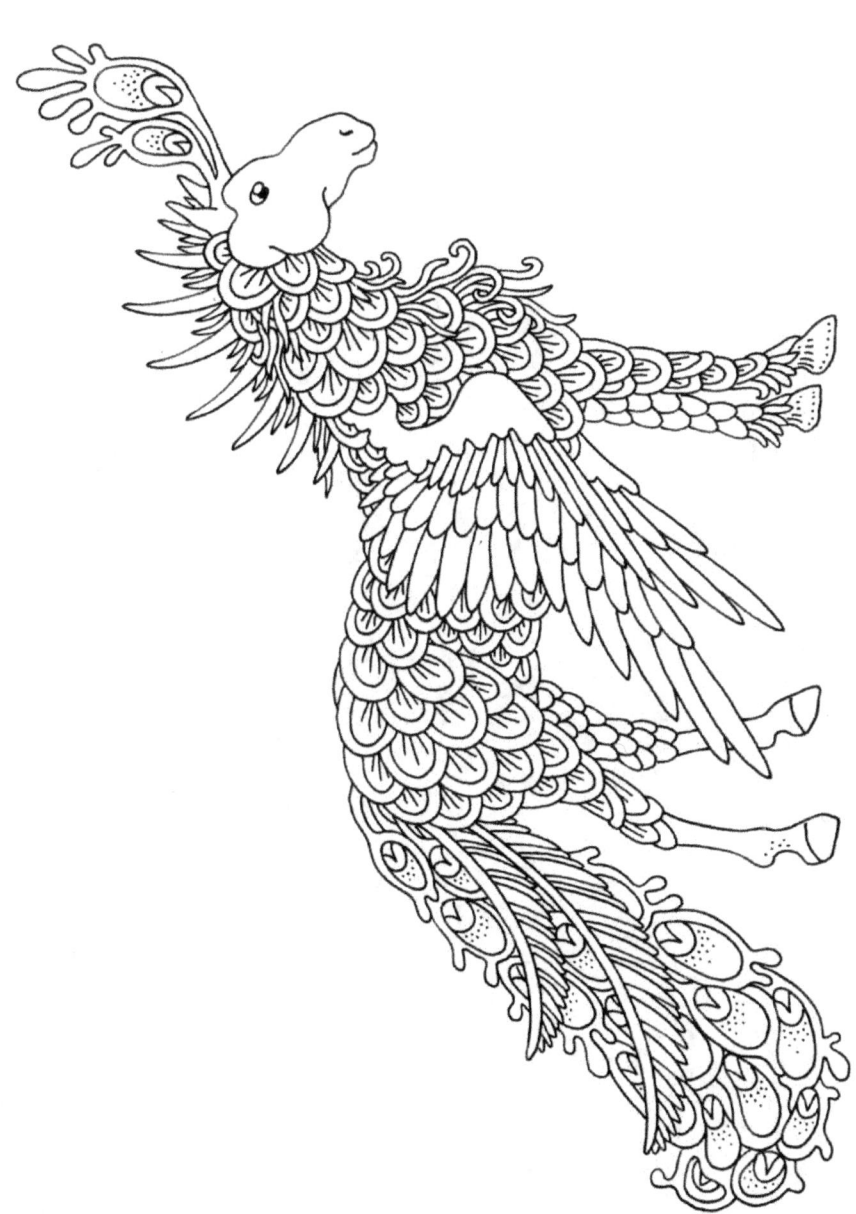

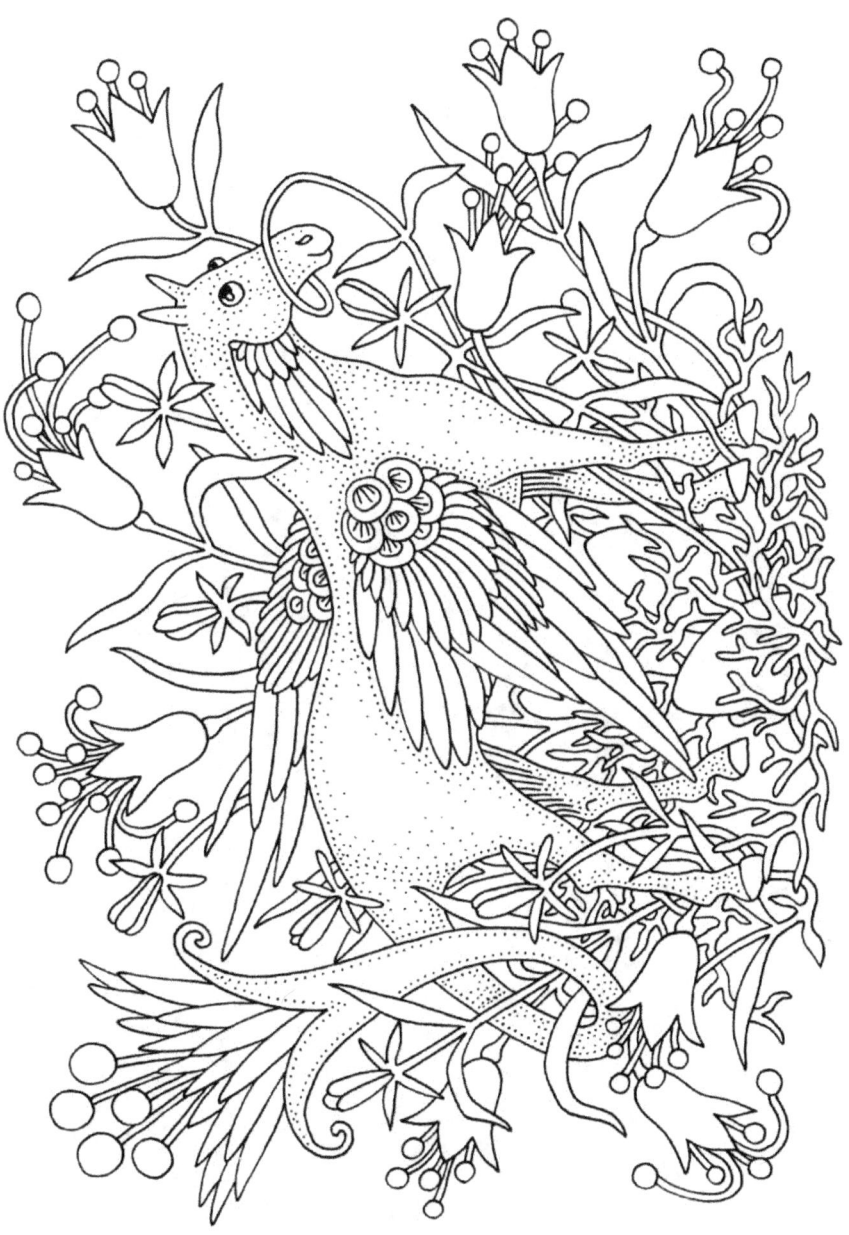

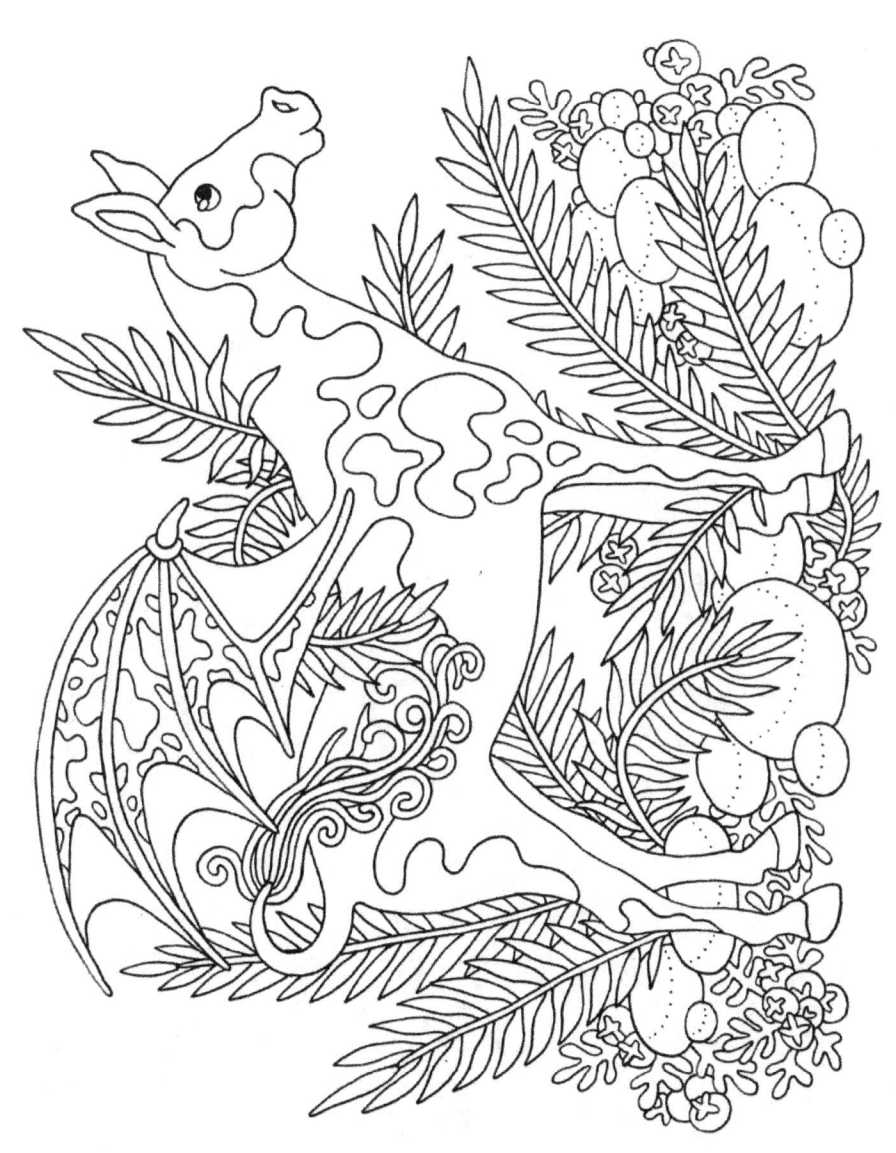

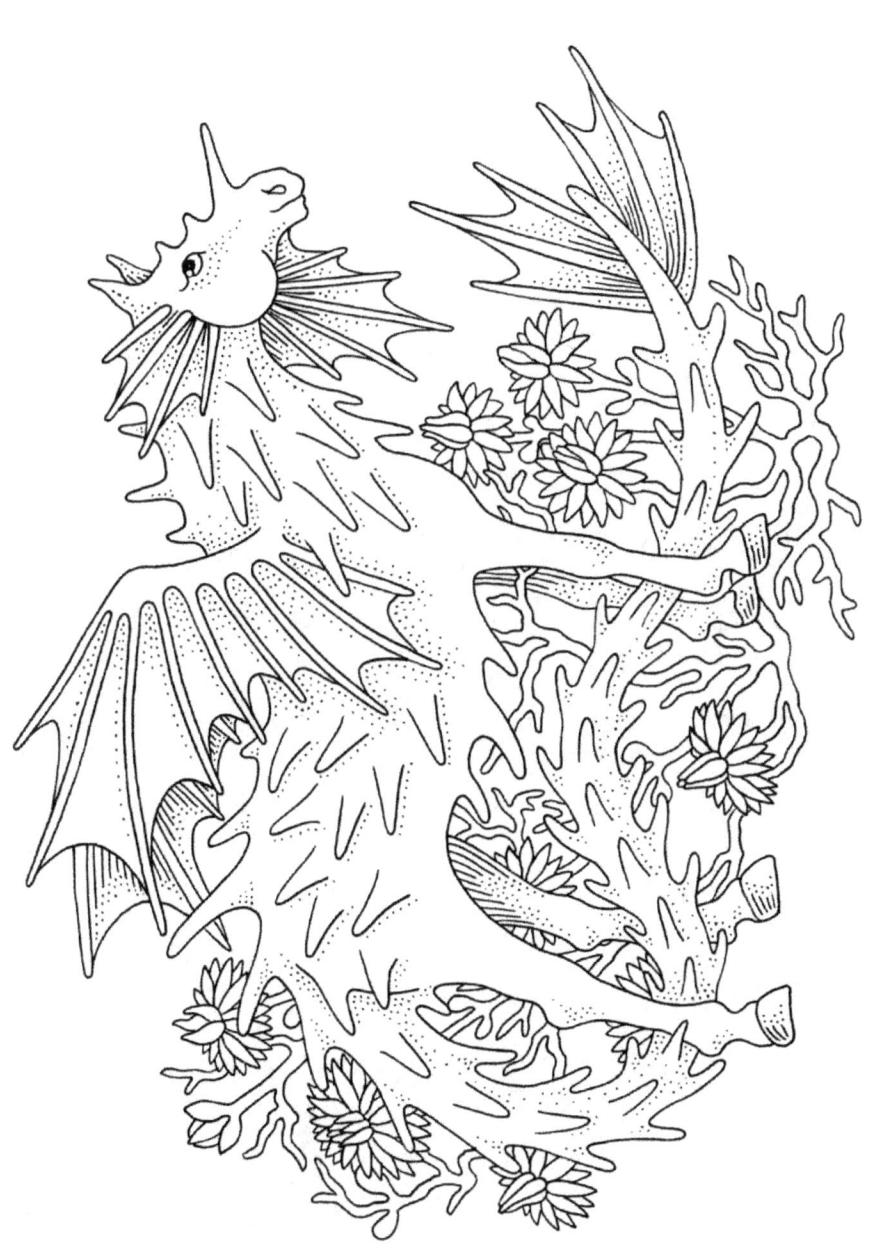

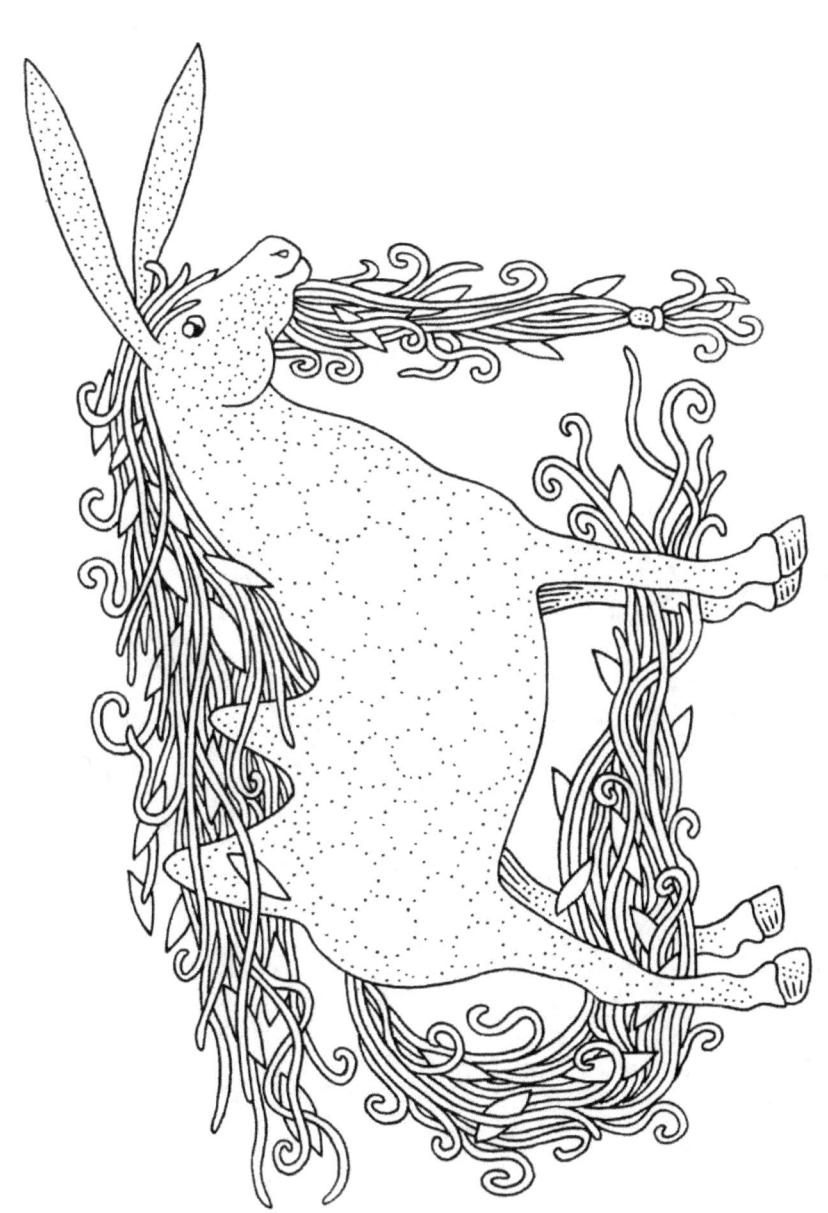

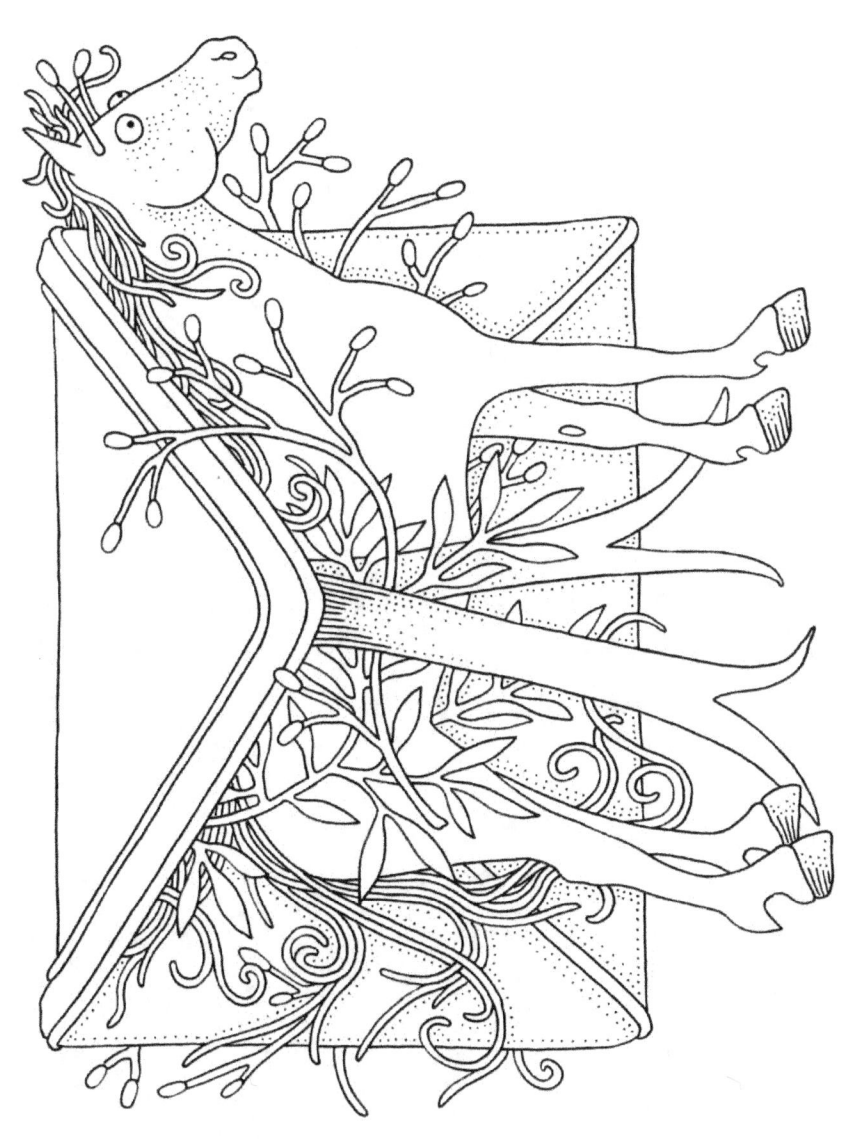

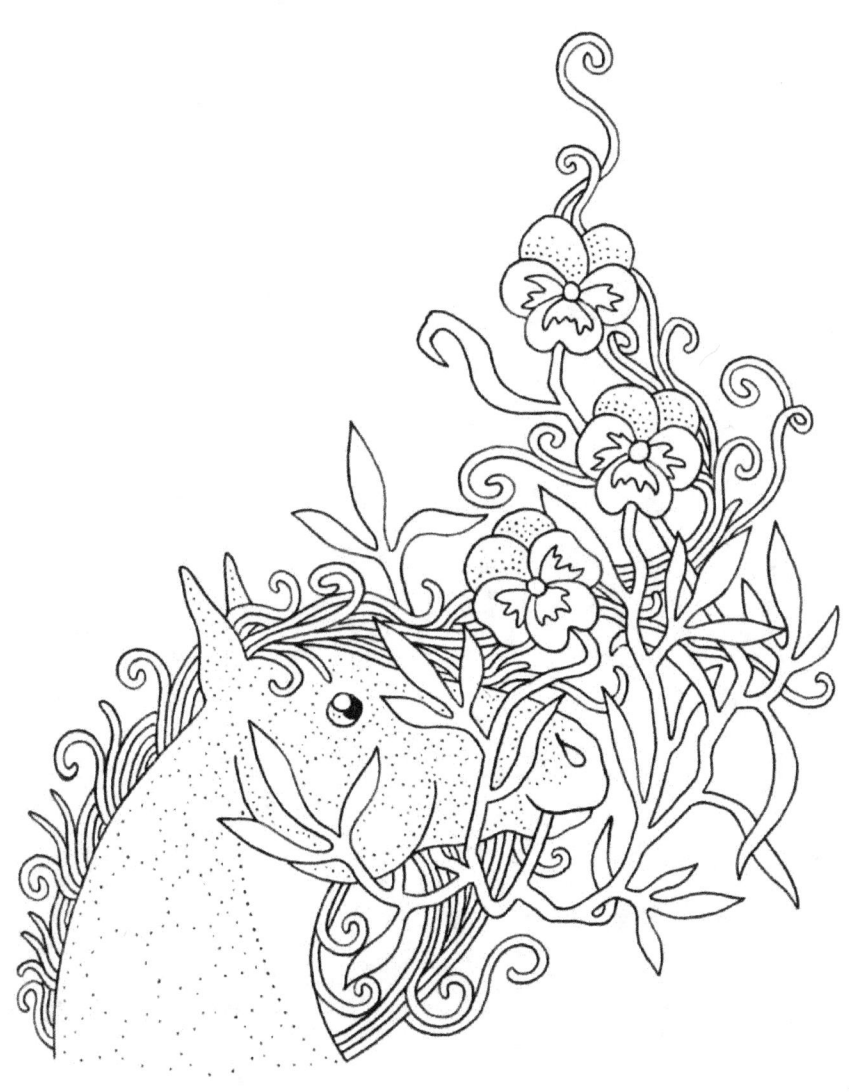